TH HEAVENLY COURTS

Elucidating The Court of Mercy and Grace, The Court of The Council of Judges, The Parliamentary Court, The Court of Times and Seasons, The International Court, The Mountains Court as well as The Supreme Court (Mount Zion).

Brigette Marx

Printed in South Africa.

First Printing, 2016

ISBN 978-0-620-72255-1
eBook ISBN 978-0-994-70160-2

www.amministries.co.za
info@amministries.co.za

Illustrator and designer: Daniëlle Scholtz
Editor: Anton F.W Alberts and Carl Roodnick

We give all honour and acknowledge the Divine guidance and inspiration of the Holy Spirit in these writings, without Whose intercession we definitely would not have been able to succeed in delivering this message.

CONTENTS

About the Author

Brigette Marx

Brigette is a seer - prophet who is zealous about the prophetic voice reaching businessmen and woman of this era. She has significant insight into the role that business people have to play in the 21st century in order to gain territory for the glory of the Kingdom of God.

Besides having an anointing for prophetic governance she has qualifications in business management. She spends most of her time sharing what she has learnt through presenting and participating in seminars, lecturing, public speaking and counselling.

Brigette has a keen ability to both see and hear in the supernatural realm. In recent times the Lord has been radically training her with respect to the Heavenly Courts and she has been provided a detailed perspective on how these courts work together, and how they align for God's glory.

Using her gift of wisdom from the Lord, she strives to continuously equip, fortify and assist in bringing prophetic alignment to the Body of Christ.

Brigette is married to Frikkie and lives with their three children, Euben, Abeygale and Anrich in Pretoria, South Africa.

SPECIAL ACKNOWLEDGMENT

"I would like to extend a special acknowledgment to Anton F.W. Alberts for his contribution to this book. I thank you and will always appreciate your efforts".

- Brigette Marx

FOREWORD

"Lord, thou hast been our dwelling place in all generations. Before the mountains were brought forth, or ever thou hadst formed the earth and the world, even from everlasting to everlasting, thou art God."

A prayer of Moses, the man of God from Psalm 90:1-2

A few years ago the Holy Spirit revealed to Brigette that heavenly courts exist and that He wants to familiarise and teach her regarding these courts.

Initially the first court revealed was the Court of Mercy and Grace and over an extended period of more than a year, she was taught, within this court, regarding the fundamentals of basic systems and procedures.

As her journey with the Holy Spirit continued, it was revealed that there were seven courts in total. The majority of her experiences referred to in this book, occurred in the company of Anton.

As such, this book is a personal account of both our respective experiences and what we have been taught by the Holy Spirit up to this point in time regarding the courts of heaven.

This writing, in essence, strives to be a core synopsis of all our relevant experiences besides information that we were led to gather on this topic, and upon which we naturally stand in unity.

As the depths of God are immeasurable at best, the information within these writings certainly do not endeavour or claim to be all inclusive.

However, the journey, thus far, has brought us immeasurable joy and so we gladly share our experiences with anyone interested in this subject.

We are privileged to have obtained wondrous knowledge and experience concerning God, the Father, His Son Jesus Christ and the Holy Spirit, which draws us with an overwhelming desire to draw even closer to Him.

So it is our wish that this book will inspire all readers to desire and develop a deeper relationship with the Holy Trinity.

We trust that you grow to love the One and only God with all of your hearts as He loves you with all of His. And may traditional mindsets, strongholds and religious systems be broken by the power of the truth of Who God is, and who you are in Christ.

May this book succeed in delivering the Good News to you, to announce the releasing of captives, to bring forth recovery of sight to those who are blind, to bring deliverance and victory to the oppressed and to establish heaven on earth in all your various spheres of influence.

Above all, may His Kingdom come; His will be done, as it is in heaven, so be it on earth.

"Now set your heart and your soul to seek the Lord your God;"

1 Chronicles 22:19

All scriptures quoted from the Bible are from the King James Version.

1

FUNDAMENTAL INFORMATION ON HEAVENLY COURTS

There are seven Heavenly Courts in the spiritual realm. The main objective of these courts are so that we can plead our cases to receive redemption, to remove the legal right from the enemy over us, receive mandates to execute specific instructions and to enable the scrolls pertaining to our lives to come to fulfilment.

While these seven courts will be discussed in more detail in chapter 3, they are called the following:

- The Court of Mercy and Grace
- The Court of the Council of Judges
- The Parliamentary Court
- The Court of Times and Seasons
- The International Court
- The Mountains Court
- The Supreme Court (Mount Zion)

Important rules of the Heavenly Courts

"And he shewed me Joshua, the high priest standing before the angel of the Lord, and Satan standing at his right hand to resist him.
And the Lord said unto Satan, The Lord rebuke thee, O Satan; even the Lord that hath chosen Jerusalem rebuke thee: is not this a brand plucked out of the fire?
Now Joshua was clothed with filthy garments, and stood before the angel.

And he answered and spake unto those that stood before him, saying, Take away the filthy garments from him. And unto him he said, Behold, I have caused thine iniquity to pass from thee, and I will clothe thee with change of raiment.
And I said, Let them set a fair mitre upon his head.So they set a fair mitre upon his head, and clothed him with garments. And the angel of the Lord stood by.
And the angel of the Lord protested unto Joshua, saying,
Thus saith the Lord of hosts; If thou wilt walk in my ways, and if thou wilt keep my charge, then thou shalt also judge my house, and shalt also keep my courts, and I will give thee places to walk among these that stand by.
Hear now, O Joshua the high priest, thou, and thy fellows that sit before thee: for they are men wondered at: for, behold, I will bring forth my servant the BRANCH."

Zechariah 3:1-8

To the best of our knowledge, together with what we have gained from our experiences we present the seven fundamental rules concerning the seven heavenly courts:

- Access to the Father and His throne will only be granted through Jesus Christ, His only begotten Son.
- Jesus Christ is the only way, truth and door through which one can enter into the courts.
- Repent of sins and transgressions before your case is presented.
- Never argue with the accuser under any circumstances, always hold your peace.
- The Word of God is the foundation for all court proceedings and verdicts, and nothing outside of the Word will stand.
- You can only appear within your jurisdictional right as certain levels of authority are required to appear in certain courts.
- The whole of creation is governed according to God's law, regardless of one's personal position towards the Creator.

It is imperative that these rules are adhered to at all times within the Heavenly Courts.

The Divine authorities in the Heavenly Courts

"Our God, His grace is remarkable, mercies are innumerable, strength is impenetrable. He is honourable, accountable and favourable.
He is unsearchable, yet knowable, indefinable, yet approachable, indescribable, yet personal.
He is beyond comprehension and further than imagination. Constant through generations, King of every nation.
My words are few and try to capture the one true God and using my own vocabulary would never do.
So He has sent His Son, Jesus Christ, Who is the image of God.
He is before all things and over all things.
He reigns.
The humble Son of God became the perfect sacrifice.
He bowed our enemy and rose in victory.
He is everything that was promised and we praise Him as the risen King, for one day He will return for us, and we will finally be united with our Saviour for eternity."

Poem by Isaac Wimberley, performed live by Brian Johnson at Kari Jobe's "Forever" concert.

The Authorities of God

- As the Father and the Judge

"And he spake a parable unto them to this end, that men ought always to pray, and not to faint;
Saying, There was in a city a judge, which feared not God, neither regarded man:

And there was a widow in that city; and she came unto him, saying, Avenge me of mine adversary. And he would not for a while: but afterward he said within himself, Though I fear not God, nor regard man;
Yet because this widow troubleth me, I will avenge her, lest by her continual coming she weary me.
And the Lord said, Hear what the unjust judge saith.
And shall not God avenge his own elect, which avenge them speedily. Nevertheless when the Son of man cometh, shall he find faith on the earth?"

Luke 18:1-8

Even a glimpse of God's majestic glory is overwhelming beyond expression. He fulfils the role of both Father and Judge, yet His heart's desire is to give us our heart's desire.

God is interested in every thought, every emotion, truly seeking communion with His children from whom He derives His greatest pleasure and joy. Eternity is not enough to fathom the depths of His heart.

Nevertheless, within our Father's heart throbs a hurt and deep sorrow due to His children's lack of love for one another. If only more people could be exposed to the gravity of the Father's heart, fewer would be so selfish with the love we are able to share. How do we even begin to presume, much less grasp His love for us, while we continue to have the audacity to show our love for one another only whenever we find it convenient?

As much as God is a righteous Father, He also needs to be fair in all His judgements.

The whole of creation is governed and regulated by the law of God and need to obey it. Operating within His own laws, God is the manifestation of the perfection of His justness.

Sometimes we are under the incorrect impression that God is not hearing nor answering in spite of our diligent fasting's and prayers, when in fact, it is the enemy's legal right held against us that prevents God from responding to our supplications.

Despite this, God has given us everything we require, through His Son, to remove any such legal right that the enemy may possess. All we need to do is apply the redeeming and saving power through the blood of Christ.

God has a heavenly counsel whom He has entrusted with specific authorities. It is written that a wise man shall attain unto wise counsel. God has such a counsel that also forms part of His trusted inner circle.

"A wise man will hear, and will increase learning; and a man of understanding shall attain unto wise counsels:"

Proverbs 1:5

You also have certain authorities within the courts at your disposal and these authorities are discussed in more detail in chapter 2.

Our Judge has a character of trust, and so the more we begin to walk and think like Jesus, the more authority He will entrust us with. He is overjoyed when we co-operate as part of His body, never expecting anything from us that He does also apply to Himself.

Every name and characteristic of God represents an authority which the Father and righteous Judge bears. This is a reflection of Who God is, and we as His children, received mercy and grace through the Son of man, to stand in these authorities.

Although it is entirely impossible to put the fullness of God's character to paper due to the sheer magnitude of His being, we can at least proclaim the following with certainty while we humbly stand in awe and admiration with our eyes fixed on Him alone.

May these words that we proclaim continually remind us of the excellence of Your nature.

You are stronger than any power in the universe;
You never change;
You are ever-present;
You are holy;
You are affectionate;
You are just;
You are infinitely wise;
You are almighty;
You are merciful;
You are eternal;
You are a shield;
You are a consuming fire;
You are the Creator;
You are the Redeemer;
You are the King of all kings;
You are the universal Father;
You are the peacekeeper;

You are a shelter;

You are always concerned;

You are the Protector;

You are the Motivator;

You are the Provider;

You are unchangeable;

You are the righteous Judge;

You are the healing power;

You are the sanctifying One;

You are flawless;

You are pure;

You are sincere;

You are honest;

You are our refuge;

You are the Rock;

You are the Saviour;

You are our relief;

You are our Shepherd.

Authorities of Jesus Christ

- As the Son of God and Mediator

"For there is one God, and one mediator between God and men, the man Christ Jesus."

1 Timothy 2:5

To be able to receive mercy and righteous judgements, we have to present our cases through our mediator, Jesus Christ. He bears various authorities within the different courts, always utilising these to assist and protect us.

"And the Lord said, Simon, Simon, behold, Satan hath desired to have you, that he may sift you as wheat:
But I have prayed for thee, that thy fail not: and when thou art converted, strengthen thy brethren."

Luke 22:31-32

Jesus intercedes and pleads before the Righteous Judge on our behalf on a continual basis. In the majority of the courts the appearance of Jesus is very true to human form, emphasising the fact that He truly is the Son of Man having come in the flesh Himself, and is able therefore, to relate to our human struggles.

He understands what it is to be tempted, to be hungry, feel pain and remorse, and so possess unimaginable compassion towards us. Jesus fights for us with passion and will do everything within His power and legal authority to make each proceeding turn in our favour.

He co-operates excellently in unity with His body. He is the proverbial example of heavenly standards, norms and principles. Jesus will never expect us to do anything which He does not do Himself. Although He knows that it would be impossible for us to uphold these standards of excellence, due to our fleshly weaknesses, He has given us the ever lingering presence of the Holy Spirit, Who enable us to walk in His Godly character through His anointing. The Son of God is the maturity of all the gifts of the Holy Spirit.

"And then shall they see the Son of man coming in a cloud with power and great glory."

Luke 21:27

The library in heaven contains uncountable scrolls pertaining to every person's life, every word spoken, every deed as well as every Godly plan and purpose for every human life, family, business, community, nation, continent and of the world. Evidently, this library also contains all the scrolls regarding every judgement delivered by God, ever.

"Who hath saved us, and called us with a holy calling, not according to our works, but according to his own purpose and grace, which was given us in Christ Jesus before the world began."

2 Timothy 1:9

An angel of the Lord showed us that within the library there is a space or room, the size of which is incomprehensible and inside are an innumerable number of doors. Each door has an inscription revealing where it leads. In the centre of the room is a door that is far bigger than the others. This door, is Jesus Christ. We are not able to navigate through the other doors before having gone through Him first.

"Then said Jesus unto them again, Verily, verily, I say unto you, I am the door of the sheep."

John 10:7

- As the High Priest

"Seeing then that we have a great high priest, that is passed into the heavens, Jesus the Son of God, let us hold fast our profession.
For we have not a high priest which cannot be touched with the feeling of our infirmities; but was in all points tempted like as we are, yet without sin.
Let us therefore come boldly unto the throne of grace, that we may obtain mercy, and find grace to help in time of need."

Hebrews 4:14-16

To better explain this position of authority of Jesus as the High Priest, we would like to relate to an experience within the Court of Mercy and Grace. This occurred in the company of someone who was not able to achieve financial breakthrough, despite continuous prayer and fasting. The accuser held a covenant, sealed with human blood, and bound between himself and one of the defendant's forefathers, giving him legal right to influence successive generations.

The defendant simply repented for the sins of the forefather and immediately the altar on which Jesus sprinkled His blood was visible. Dressed in a priestly garment, Jesus presented His blood as a testimony, which in turn destroyed the power of the covenant the accuser had in his possession.
God declared a new covenant between Himself and the defendant as well as the generations to follow and sealed it with the blood of Christ.

"And I heard a loud voice saying in heaven, Now is come salvation, and strength, and the Kingdom of our God, and the power of His Christ: for the accuser of his brethren is cast down, which accused them before our God day and night.
And they overcame him by the blood of the Lamb, and by the word of their testimony; and they loved not their lives unto the death."

Revelation 12:10-11

As High Priest, Jesus also presents the bowl of incense containing all our prayers.

- As the Good Shepherd

"I am the good shepherd: the good shepherd giveth his life for the sheep."

John 10:11

Jesus received the authority to protect us by giving the greatest sacrifice of all, His life, for us. This gives Jesus an advantage in the heavenly courts over the enemy that he will never be able to diminish.

Jesus has the heart of a shepherd, by which He wants to care for, guide, and protect His flock (the Church). His compassion for us is beyond human comprehension and His grief over our afflictions is testimony to that.

In spite of the heartache He has to endure when we go through trials and tribulations His love for us is such, that He allows these tests, so that we may build character, grow in faith, learn to overcome through faith and mature in Him.

This He allows solely for our benefit, and when we persevere the rewards will far outweigh the afflictions.

"Therefore seeing we have this, as we have received mercy, we faint not;"

2 Corinthians 4:1

"For our light affliction, which is but for a moment, worketh for us a far more exceeding and eternal weight of glory;"

2 Corinthians 4:17

- As the King of Kings and Lord of Lords

"These shall make war with the Lamb, and the Lamb shall overcome them: for he is Lord of lords, and King of kings: and they that are with him are called, and chosen, and faithful."

Revelation 17:14

Jesus, blessed, only Sovereign, ruler of the kings of the earth, mighty and awesome God whose loving – kindness is everlasting. Unto Him is given all authority and might to reign over all the earth and all the heavens. Every knee shall bow and every tongue shall confess that Jesus Christ is the King of kings and the Lord of all.

Although Jesus has the right to stand in His authority as King and Lord over all, it will most assuredly always be directed against the enemy to further assist us with protection.

This is a great example of how a position of authority is used to serve, rather than manipulate, dominate, and intimidate

- As Judge

"And I saw heaven opened, and behold, a white horse, and he that sat upon him was called Faithful and True, and in righteousness He doth judge and make war.
His eyes were as a flame of fire, and on His head were many crowns; and he had a name written, that no man knew, but he himself.
And he was clothed with a vesture dipped in blood: and His name is called The Word of God.
And the armies which were in heaven followed him upon white horses, clothed in fine linen, white and clean.
And out of his mouth goeth a sharp sword, that with it he should smite the nations: and he shall rule them with a rod of iron: and he treadeth the winepress of the fierceness and wrath of Almighty God.
And he hath on his vesture and on his thigh a name written, KING OF KINGS AND LORD OF LORDS."

Revelation 19:11-16

It is through the delivering power of the blood of the Lamb that God's children can be forgiven for sins and vindicated. Jesus Christ, the Judge, conquered death and rose from the grave.

He shed His blood so that those who choose to receive Him as Lord and Saviour may be delivered from eternal damnation. Through His sacrifice the children of the Light can now receive redemption from the curse of death and the struggles we have with iniquities.

By God's appointment the rule and dominion over all governments and powers rests on the shoulders of His Son, Jesus Christ and therefore, like God, He also exercises judgement.

Jesus as judge is more prominent in some courts than others. We therefore proclaim, that Jesus will stand in the fullness of His authority on the day of judgement, when every tongue shall confess that He is Lord and every knee will bow to Him.

Authorities of the Holy Spirit

"And the spirit of the LORD shall rest upon him, the spirit of wisdom and understanding, the spirit of counsel and might, the spirit of knowledge and of the fear of the LORD."

Isaiah 11:2

The procedures and proceedings in all the courts are orchestrated by the Holy Spirit. Without the guidance and gifts of the Holy Spirit it would be impossible to navigate within the heavenly courts.

Not only does the Holy Spirit guide one in the courts, but He ensures that everyone present remains in one accord and in perfect harmony with the perfect will of God.

The Spirit gives you wisdom to supplicate in harmony with the sovereign will of God. Should words fail you, He will inspire you, and may even testify on your behalf. He is the ultimate supporter in need and your strength when you yourself fail. The Spirit of God is the power in every word spoken by God.

In an attempt to specifically smother that which God has ordained to be birthed within every decade, various occult groups perform rituals and speak curses over that decade.

An astonishing event took place during a recent experience in court in the company of the founder of a ministry that was founded in South Africa in the early 90's. The aim was to align the ministry with God's plan and purpose.

While proceedings were under way and parties involved presented their cases, the enemy's contention was that occult rituals and curses performed at the beginning of the decade in which the ministry had been found, gave him legal right to destroy every Godly ordained ministry (church and business).

The Spirit revealed that some ministries had already been destroyed in the "womb", whereas others had become monuments or statues. In other words, they had become distant memories of something great that once existed.

Jesus then presented every righteous prayer that was prayed on behalf of those ministries as evidence against the enemy's case. This activated the overcoming power of the blood of the Lamb which in turn gave God the right to move on behalf of those ministries.

The Holy Spirit then moved like a mighty wind across South Africa and blew new life into every ministry that was established during that particular decade, releasing new strength, revival and might.

What started as an exercise to address the concerns of one ministry, in the end, benefitted the country.

"This is he that came by water and blood, even Jesus Christ; not by water only, but by water and blood. And it is the Spirit that beareth witness, because the Spirit is truth. For there are three that bear record in heaven, the Father, the Word and the Holy Ghost: and these three are one.
And there are three that bear witness in earth, the Spirit and the water, and the blood: and these three agree in one."

1 John 5:6-7

Authorities of the books and scrolls

"I beheld till the thrones were cast down, and the Ancient of days did sit, whose garment was as white as snow, and the hair of his head like the pure wool: his throne was like the fiery flame, and his wheels as burning fire.
A fiery stream issued and came forth from before him: thousand thousands ministered unto him, and ten thousand times ten thousand stood before him: the judgement was set, and the books were opened."

Daniel 7: 9-10

Before the foundations of the earth were formed, God had already written a book containing the predestined purpose, plan and design for all continents, nations, countries, governments, cities, communities, businesses, ministries and individuals.

During court proceedings the relevant book pertaining to a specific area of influence is opened and God renders decisions based on what is written in a particular book or scroll.

"For we are his workmanship, created in Christ Jesus unto good works, which God hath before ordained that we should walk in them."

Ephesians 2:10

Prophets are of great importance within the courts of heaven as the prophecies they prophecy are from these books of heaven. Judgement will not be rendered until such time as that which is written in these books are declared or prayed.

"Surely the Lord GOD will do nothing, but he revealeth his secret unto his servants the prophets."

Amos 3:7

Prophets should always make an asserted effort to reach Mount Zion (the Holy Mountain) within the spiritual realm, to be in close proximity to the Lord's presence for Him to be willing to release the relevant revelations to them.

In order to successfully navigate within the seven heavenly courts, one would need the anointed prophets of the Lord to seek out whatever is written in the books which in turn will serve as guidance to God's purpose and plan. This will allow for that which is written in the spiritual dimension to be integrated with the physical dimension so that God's Kingdom is established on earth.

It is of great importance that the children of God remain obedient and move according to His will, once such a prophecy (that which is written in the books) is released over them.

It will be utterly fruitless to expect the prophecies to come to fulfilment if one does not use one's authority in obedience to God's ultimate plan and purpose. Most importantly, we need to keep moving forward and to press on to even greater accomplishments.

Although some prophets receive a specific anointing to bring vision and purpose; and although the Lord uses them powerfully to position the Church, and reveal that which is written; it is an even greater responsibility for each and every child of His to stand in an intimately personal relationship with the Father, so that He may make His plan and purpose known to him or her also.

"And hath made of one blood all nations of men for to dwell on all the face of the earth, and hath determined the times before appointed, and the bounds of their habitation;"

Acts 17:26

"Thine eyes did see my substance, yet being unperfect; and in thy book all my members were written, which in continuance were fashioned, when as yet there was none of them."

Psalm 139:16

As mentioned earlier, various books are written for different purposes and we will never be able to remotely comprehend the magnitude of this fact. That said, through revelation from the Holy Spirit, the Lord revealed that He had personally written a foreword, for each and every book or scroll.

Our God is a God of personal relationships and detail, being wholeheartedly interested in every aspect of our lives. The Lord Almighty derives the greatest pleasure from having communion with His children.

The Lord being personally responsible for every foreword, does however, reveal a little about the extent of the compassion in His heart.

What follows is a foreword written in the scroll for a specific business, that was revealed by the Holy Spirit for that particular business. It is followed by a prayer Jesus delivered before the creation of the earth:

The Father:

"I have chosen you and you will reflect my heart towards the nations.

You will be like a tree that was planted by streams of water and one that carries good fruit at the right times. I have anointed you as king on My holy mountain, Zion.

You will not fear the tens of thousands that will rise up against thee and when you call I shall heed to that call. Sacrifice offerings of righteousness and trust in Me.

Through you I will make an end to the wickedness of the unrighteous and through you will I establish righteousness on earth. I shall favour you with my blessings and crown you with a crown of fine gold.

You will trust in Me and by My grace you will not falter. You will expect Me and will therefore never stand ashamed. You will remain faithful and I will make My ways known to you. Your hope will remain in My Word and I shall deliver you from injustices, Myself.

When your strength leaves you, you will bring your supplications before Me, and I shall listen and respond to the lamentations of your heart.
I shall never leave you and will always provide instant help in your time of need. I am your Shepherd and you shall not want.

Excellence and favour will follow you all the days of your life and you will dwell in the House of your Father for all eternity. Your hart will be My hart and you will not eat from the table of those that dabble in wickedness. You will be called, salvation, and you will be a beacon of hope to multitudes. Silver and gold belong to you, and My gates are being opened for you.

You will honour Me, yes, you that have the breath of life, will praise Me."

By reading this one cannot resist but be immensely aware, not only of God's grandeur, but also His absolute authority. In spite of His loving kindness He is most certainly not to be trifled with.

The Son:

"Heavenly Father, I pray for them, so they may be protected in their hour of temptation and tribulation. That they may not be destroyed by the enemy and remain standing. Father, I ask that you bestow mercy and grace upon them, that so diligently want to build My Kingdom. Forget them not, Father, and keep them within Your heart. Guard them with Your loving kindness and shelter them under Your wings.

I shall teach and educate them in Your ways and I ask that You look upon Me, when they fail. I also ask that you not hold them accountable for these sins. Support them with Your right hand and provide in their needs in abundance so they may be able to give without having to take. Make them the head, and not the tail.

This is My will, as it is Your will. I shall build My image in them because I know it will please You.

Please bring My sacrifice into remembrance when the enemy accuses them and let your wrath not ignite against them.

I am strong in their weaknesses and I thank You that You have given Me the power to wipe away their sins and transgressions so that they may be purified and sanctified by Me to stand in victory.

Protect them that You have entrusted to Me, dear Father, so that they may not be lost."

This prayer emphasizes the absolute compassion and endearment that Jesus is willing to bestow upon all His children.

- The book about the life of Jesus

Just as the Lord has written books regarding the plans and purposes for our lives, a book was written about Jesus Christ and the plans and purposes God had for Him.

"Wherefore when he cometh into the world, he saith, Sacrifice and offering thou wouldest not, but a body hast thou prepared me:
In burnt offerings and sacrifices for sin thou hast had no pleasure.
Then said I, Lo, I come (in the volume of the book it is written of me) to do they will, O God."

Hebrew 10:5-7

- The book of life

"And I saw the dead, small and great, stand before God; and the books were opened: and another book was opened, which is the book of life: and the dead were judged out of those things which were written in the books, according to their works."

Revelation 20:12

The book of life (also called the Lamb's book of life) contains the names of all those who have overcome adversity and who have inherited eternal life.

"He that overcometh, the same shall be clothed in white raiment; and I will not blot out his name out of the book of life, but I will confess his name before my Father, and before his angels."

Revelation 3:5

A life of holiness and purity needs to be lived through the redeeming power of the blood of the Lamb, in order for one's name to be written in the book of life.

The book of Revelation in the Bible is very adamant that those whose names are not written in the book of life will be thrown into the lake of fire during the great white throne judgement.

This life of holiness and purity is not on our terms, but on God's. That is why He revealed His Word to us; so that our woeful ignorance can never be uttered as an excuse.

"And there shall in no wise enter into it any thing that defileth, neither whatsoever worketh abomination, or maketh a lie: but they which are written in the Lamb's book of life."

Revelation 21:27

- The book of remembrance

This book documents every honourable word ever spoken of the Lord; besides every blessing and scripture ever proclaimed by us in truth. In addition, it chronicles every faithful act of service for the Lord, every encouraging word, every unselfish deed, every sacrifice we made, and all the persecutions we suffered for the Lord.

Whatever is written in the book of remembrance is used as testimony within the courts for the whole of creation to see.

"Then they that feared the LORD spake often one to another: and the LORD hearkened, and heard it, and a book of remembrance was written before him for them that feared the LORD, and that thought upon his name"

Malachi 3:16

During a recent visit in the heavenly courts for a specific business, when we enquired of the Lord whether the foundations of that business were built upon His word and Jesus Christ, Jesus as the Mediator opened the book of remembrance.

Every single word that was spoken or proclaimed through scriptures, blessings and prophecy from when the foundations were laid, were used as testimony for this particular business, serving as proof that the foundations were indeed laid upon the Word.

- The book of destinies

In this book is written all the destinies that are pre – ordained for the many nations, their leaders as well as the people within those nations and from these written destinies judgements will be rendered.

"And the voice which I heard from heaven spake unto me again, and said, Go and take the little book which is open in the hand of the angel which standeth upon the sea and upon the earth.
And I went unto the angel, and said unto him, Give me the little book.
And he said unto me, Take it, and eat it up; and it shall make thy belly bitter, but it shall be in thy mouth sweet as honey.
And I took the little book out of the angel's hand, and ate it up; and it was in my mouth sweet as honey: and as soon as I had eaten it, my belly was bitter.
And he said unto me, Thou must prophesy again before many peoples, and nations, and tongues and kings."

Revelation 10:8-11

A similar event took place in Ezekiel chapter 3, where the Lord gave Ezekiel a scroll (same as books in Biblical terms) to eat, and then instructed him to prophecy over Israel. As the prophet ate the scroll, the words that were written on the scroll were imparted to his spirit, enabling him to prophecy accordingly.

In Ezekiel chapter 37, the Lord took Ezekiel to a valley which was full of dry bones and asked him whether the bones could live. Ezekiel answered by saying: *"the Lord knowest."*
The Lord commanded him to prophecy over the dry bones and the moment that happened, the judgement was rendered, a verdict was delivered, and God was able to raise an entire army from the valley full of dry bones.

God moves through the heavenly prophecies that prophets boldly release on earth.

"Thou tellest my wanderings: put thou my tears into thy bottle: are they not in thy

book?"

Psalm 56:8

- The flying scrolls

"Then I turned, and lifted up mine eyes, and looked, and behold a flying roll.
And he said unto me, What seest thou? And I answered, I see a flying roll; the length thereof is twenty cubits, and the breadth thereof ten cubits.
Then said he unto me, This is the curse that goeth forth over the face of the whole earth: for every one that stealeth shall be cut off as on this side according to it; and every one that sweareth shall be cut off as on that side according to it.
I will bring it forth, saith the LORD of hosts, and it shall enter into the house of the thief, and into the house of him that sweareth falsely by my name: and it shall remain in the midst of his house, and shall consume it with the timber thereof and the stones thereof."

Zechariah 5:1-4

Once a judgement is rendered, a scroll containing this judgement is released and this is exactly what Zechariah saw. Flying scrolls are the judgements that have not yet landed and are therefore not coming into fulfilment on earth. Once these scrolls land, justice is done.

In order to maintain righteousness, God uses apostles and prophets to see and declare judgements. For a particular judgement to manifest on earth, a declaration needs to be executed after being rendered during a court case.

Those standing in apostolic or prophetic authority should then ask the Holy Spirit to reveal these flying scrolls, and take up their positions to land these verdicts on earth.

Authorities of the various Testimonies

Despite Satan or his cohort always being the accuser, there are many powerful witnesses that may be called upon to testify.

The various testimonies that testify on your behalf within the Heavenly Courts include, but are not necessarily limited to:

- The Blood of the Lamb
- The Cloud of Witnesses
- The Water
- Prayer
- The Word of God
- Decrees
- Contracts
- Covenants

The following are brief descriptions and explanations of those testimonies that were revealed to us, to date:

- The Blood of the Lamb

"And to Jesus the mediator of the new covenant, and to the blood of sprinkling, that speaketh better things than that of Abel."

Hebrews 12:24

The scripture above reveals that the blood of Christ speaks better things than that of human's sacrifice. Two things are important to understand from this:

Blood speaks. And as such, it has a voice, with which you need to answer every accusation the Accuser brings against you, through the blood of the Lamb.

The blood of Jesus holds greater authority than any other blood sacrifice.

Jesus laid down His life on the Altar to bring His blood as the perfect and complete sacrifice. His blood will forever have a greater power within the spiritual dimension.

For those who are willing to accept and apply the power of His blood, it has authority over every demonic force, any blood sacrifice or covenant.

"And almost all things are by the law purged with blood; and without shedding of blood is no remission."

Hebrews 9:22

One drop of our Saviour's blood has enough power to cleanse and save an entire nation, and through His blood, the following are made possible:

You are purified and sanctified.

"Wherefore Jesus also, that he might sanctify the people with his own blood, suffered without the gate."

Hebrews 13:12

You are redeemed.

"Neither by the blood of goats and calves, but by His own blood he entered in once into the holy place, having obtained eternal redemption for us."

Hebrews 9:12

You are healed.

"Who his own self bare our sins in his own body on the tree, that we, being dead to sins, should live unto righteousness: by whose stripes ye were healed."

1 Peter 2:24

You are justified and saved.

"Much more then, being now justified by his blood, we shall be saved from the wrath through him."

Romans 5:9

- Your sins are forgiven.

"In whom we have redemption through his blood, even the forgiveness of sins:"

Colossians 1:14

You receive boldness to go approach the Father's Throne of mercy and grace.

"Having therefore, brethren, boldness to enter into the holiest by the blood of Jesus,"

Hebrews 10:19

You receive power and authority to overcome.

"And they overcame him by the blood of the Lamb, and by the word of their testimony; and they loved not their lives unto death."

Revelation 12:11

You receive eternal life.

"The Jews therefore strove among themselves, saying, How can this man give us his flesh to eat?
Then Jesus said unto them. Verily, verily, I say unto you, Except ye eat the flesh of the Son of man, and drink his blood, ye have no life in you.
Whoso eateth my flesh, and drinketh my blood, hath eternal life; and I will raise him up at the last day.
For my flesh is meat indeed, and my blood is drink indeed.
He that eateth my flesh, and drinketh my blood, dwelleth in me, and I in him."

John 6:52-56

- The Cloud of Witnesses

"And these all, having obtained a good report through faith, received not the promise: God having provided some better thing for us, that they without us should not be made perfect."

Hebrews 11:39-40

"Wherefore seeing we also are compassed about with so great a cloud of witnesses, let us lay aside every weight, and the sin which doth so easily beset us, and let us run with patience the race that is set before us,"

Hebrews 12:1

Paul writes about the great men and woman of faith who walked the earth in Hebrews 11. In chapter 12 he then continues discussing the cloud of witnesses and in verse 23 refers to them as: *"the spirits of just men made perfect."*

From these scriptures it is evident that the Cloud of Witnesses refers to people who have died, but are now with the Lord in Heaven. It is important to remember that the Cloud of Witness operate through their own free will or a request by the Holy Trinity and cannot be summoned otherwise. They have a very specific function within the Kingdom of God.

In innumerable cases, this Cloud of Witnesses, testified on behalf of the living as they possess an insatiable desire to have God's Kingdom established on earth. They want you to stand in victory with regards to your calling, as they cannot be made perfect without you.

Building takes place on foundations they established, and harvests are reaped, which they have planted. The Cloud of Witnesses will surely be rewarded for the works performed by the earthly children of God. These rewards will be given on the Day of the Lord when the final judgement will be rendered.

Everything revolves around the expansion and establishment of God's Kingdom and the love we have for Him and one another. They will therefore, pray and intercede for you, testify on your behalf, plead for you, release blessings over you and empower you, by sharing their authorities and anointing with you. This they will execute with tremendous passion given their love for Almighty God and His Church.

"To the general assembly and church of the firstborn, which are written in heaven, and to God the Judge of all, and to the spirits of just men made perfect."

Hebrews 12:23

During an experience within the Court of Mercy and Grace, King

David himself pleaded on behalf of a businessman who was in court, as well as all others on earth, blessed with the same anointing as himself, praying the following:

"Lord, I plead with You today, that the authority that I have established on earth, live through this child of Yours and all others that are blessed with this authority. I ask Lord, that You protect him, like You protected me when I dwelled the earth. I pray that You provide for him, like You provided for me, and that You will deliver him from his enemies, like You delivered me from them that persecuted me. I also ask that You bestow upon him the same favour, grace and mercy which You bestowed upon me. Amen."

- The Water

"This is he that came by water and blood, even Jesus Christ; not by water only, but by water and blood. And it is the spirit that beareth witness, because the Spirit is truth. For there are three that bear record in heaven, the Father, the Word, and the Holy Ghost: and these three are one.
And there are three that bear witness in earth, the spirit, and the water, and the blood: and these three agree in one."

1 John 5:6-8

Contrary to the general notion that the significance of water only testifies for us through baptism, a recent experience we had in The Court of Mercy and Grace provided proof of the existence of other testimonies around the spiritual meaning and application of water:

The case involved a businessman whose business owned a few branches throughout South Africa. In order to establish a Holy Altar over his business many hours were spent in praise and worship at the head office.

It was revealed that curses by satanic groups, were literally written in the ground in front of each branch. The enemy used these curses to obtain a legal right supposedly to instigate violence and severe rebellion against the business.

Being somewhat perplexed, as this accusation was a totally new experience for us, we enquired of the Holy Spirit how we should defend ourselves against this.

The Holy Spirit answered and instructed us to use the power in the water which flowed from the Holy Altar to bear witness for the business and cleanse the ground.

Holy Altars are erected through prayer, praise and worship, studying and declaring the Word of God and by fasting.

A porthole is created which grants us access to heaven when a Holy Altar is erected. Streams of living waters flows from this Altar, bearing witness on our behalf.

The moment we presented the testimony of the water, it moved in waves over all the branches, cleansing the ground of the curses.

Shortly after this court case, it became clear that the enemy had already taken the necessary steps to prepare for a violent outbreak, as a situation arose which had the potential to unleash great calamity, but was hindered from occurring due to this intercession. We praised God for His faithfulness.

- Prayers

"Let my prayer be set forth before thee as incense; and the lifting up of my hands as the evening sacrifice."

Psalm 141:2

Every prayer prayed in faith is like incense going up to heaven in sacrifice, and is captured forever. These are the prayers of faithful children of God, causing judgements from The Courts of Heaven to be rendered. These rendered judgements save souls, produces healing, opens doors, releases mercy and victoriously empowers the church to overcome opposition.

Daniel made his supplications known to God in prayer and fasting. He understood from the prophecy of Jeremiah that the Israelites would be freed from captivity by King Darius after seventy years.
Had Daniel not prayed and supplicated on behalf of Israel, it is likely they would have remained in captivity for a longer period. Never underestimate the power of the sincere and earnest prayer of the righteous.

"In the first year of his reign I Daniel understood by books the number of the years, whereof the word of the Lord came to Jeremiah the prophet, that he would accomplish seventy years in the desolations of Jerusalem.
And I set my face unto the Lord God, to seek by prayer and supplications, with fasting, and sackcloth, and ashes:
And I prayed unto the Lord my God, and made my confession, and said, O Lord, the great and dreadful God, keeping the mercy and covenant to them that love him, and to them that keep his commandments;"

Daniel 9:2-4

We have also had an experience, where we had to present our case in the Judge's chambers, as we did not yet have permission to enter that specific court.

In the chambers, a silhouette of the Father was visible, with Jesus being literally one with the Father. This also made it possible for us to comprehend the concept of three persons being in One God. God, through Jesus, revealed Himself in a manner that made it possible for us to bear His presence.

The Lord continuously paced up and down while we presented our case. He contemplated what we had to say, considering everything and everyone involved.

At the same time, angels constantly entered into the chambers with reports, and were also handed additional tasks. These tasks did not solely revolve around the matters of the earth, but all of creation.

The Lord then asked all those present what the intents of their hearts were. When the Creator of the universe asks you such a sudden and unexpected question, then you begin to understand what it means to have the fear of the Lord. It is simply overwhelming, to say the least.

It is not possible to lie to Almighty God as He already knows what is in your heart. We later realised that the true test of this exercise was not to merely to determine what the intents of our hearts were, but rather, whether we were going to be totally sincere, and answer with the whole truth.

It is quite intimidating to answer a difficult question truthfully, when you know that the One asking the question, already knows the whole truth. This experience reminds one of the tragic story of Ananias and Sapphira's dishonesty recorded in Acts chapter 5 verse 1-11.

After we truthfully answered the Lord's question, an opportunity was presented where all the prayers of God's' children could be heard simultaneously within a moment.

A multitude of voices rose from earth to heaven, with some being somewhat louder than others. The Holy Spirit then revealed that those voices which were louder, were from those who are truly persevering.

The following happens when God's children persevere in their prayer lives:

- judgements are released on earth
- individuals and families are saved
- people receive a second chance in life
- angelic armies are released
- the Father hears every word uttered in faith.

There have been experiences where businesses have struggled to obtain certain government contracts due to satanic rituals done over an area or city. This is one of the modus operandi by which the enemy gains territory.

It is therefore amazing to witness how the power in the prayers of children of God raises up Holy Altars in those areas and cities in which they live. Jesus then presents these prayers in Court, which in turn gives God the legal right to take back an area or city from the enemy.

Judgements are released, demanding that righteousness be done to the righteous. Contracts are released to righteous businesses through the authority from heaven to gain territory, as the whole Body of Christ stands in victory by working together in unity and harmony.

Therefore, it is quite possible to be co – responsible for changing the world whilst being completely unaware of the fact.

"Be careful for nothing; but in every thing by prayer and supplication with thanksgiving let your requests be made known unto God. And the peace of God, which passeth all understanding, shall keep your hearts and minds through Christ Jesus."

Philippians 4:6-7

- The Word of God

"In the beginning was the Word, and the Word was with God, and the Word was God.
The same was in the beginning with God.
All things were made by him; and without him was not any thing made that was made.
In him was life; and the life was the light of men.
And the light shineth in darkness; and the darkness comprehended it not."

John 1:1-5

Nothing in the Heavenly Courts can stand outside the Word of God, and nothing can successfully resist the Word of God. The Word is the foundation for and root for of all truth, and nothing will remain standing which is not built upon Jesus Christ, the Word of God.

The enemy is not allowed to present any accusation or hold any legal right which stands outside the Word of God.

A very interesting case in question, emphasizing this fact, involved the educational system in South Africa within the Parliamentary Court. The kingdom of darkness, opposing us, used the following scripture to state their case:

"Let every soul be subject unto the higher powers. For there is no power but of God: the powers that be are ordained of God.
Whosoever therefore resisteth the power, resisteth the ordinance of God: and they that resist shall receive themselves the damnation."

Romans 13:1-2

The aim of the enemy was for us to surrender to their governmental authority, which they received, solely because God had permitted it.

A representative of the Kingdom of God, with jurisdictional authority over South Africa, then boldly stood up and proclaimed that we still possessed greater authority, because He who is in us is greater than he who is in the world.

"Ye are of God, little children, and have overcome them: because greater is he that is in you, than he that is in the world."

1 John 4:4

In addition, the enemy brought an argument that they had a legal right over the children because God gave them the right to visit the sins of the forefathers upon the third and fourth generations of them that do not obey and love Him.

"Thou shalt not bow down thyself to them, nor serve them: for I the LORD thy God am a jealous God, visiting the iniquity of the fathers upon the children unto the third and fourth generation of them that hate me;"

Exodus 20:5

We then opposed this argument with the next verse, proclaiming:

"And shewing mercy unto thousands of them that love me, and keep my commandments."

Exodus 20:6

We asked the Lord to bring into remembrance those within South Africa who truly love and abide in Him, both the living and those who have passed on to be with the Lord. And furthermore, through His promise, to bless our children, and to remove the enemy's stronghold on the educational system of the country. We also pleaded with the Lord to establish His will within this particular sphere of influence. The enemy's arguments were overruled, and our requests granted.

- Decrees

"And they overcame him by the blood of the Lamb, and by the word of their testimony; and they loved not their lives unto the death."

Revelation 12:11

Every word spoken or written is a declaration, contract, covenant, blessing or curse and because it is legally binding it influences everything that takes place on earth.

The words of our testimony advances either the Kingdom of God or the kingdom of the enemy. The following words from King Solomon underlines this truth:

"Death and life are in the power of the tongue: and they that love it shall eat the fruit thereof."

Proverbs 18:21

There are two types of decrees, those spoken, and those written. Let's take a look at the spoken decrees first.

"This book of the law shall not depart out of thy mouth; but thou shalt meditate therein day and night, that thou mayest observe to do according to all that is written therein: for then thou shalt make thy way prosperous, and then thou shalt have good success."

Joshua 1:8

The Lord commanded Joshua to meditate on, and proclaim His word. Joshua's mind had to be aligned with the Word in order for him to decree it.

These declarations released heavenly judgements over the enemies of Israel, while empowering Joshua and the Israelite army to overcome their enemies and possess the promise land.

The battle had already been won in the spiritual realm through the decrees that were spoken, and the fear of the Lord manifested itself physically in the enemy, by them simply hearing about the God of Israel and His awesome power.

"And she said unto the men, I know that the LORD hath given you the land, and that your terror is fallen upon us, and that all the inhabitants of the land faint because of you.

For we have heard how the LORD dried up the water of the Red sea for you, when

ye came out of Egypt; and what ye did unto the two kings of the Amorites, that were on the other side of Jordan, Sihon and Og, whom ye utterly destroyed.
And as soon as we heard these things, our hearts did melt, neither did there remain any more courage in any man, because of you: for the Lord your God, he is God in heaven above, and in earth beneath."

Joshua 2:9-11

Keeping in mind that everything in the physical dimension is a reflection of the spiritual dimension written decrees may be explained as follows:

"Woe unto them that decree unrighteous decrees, and that write grievousness which they have prescribed;"

Isaiah 10:1

In the Bible there is an excellent example of the execution of a written decree in the book of Esther:

Under the influence of the murderous Haman, King Ahasuerus agreed to the elimination of every Jew, both young and old, to be effected in one day. There was great mourning among the Jews when a copy of the king's decree, commanding his will, was delivered to all his various provinces.
Encouraged by her uncle Mordecai, Queen Esther, supplicated on behalf of the Jews before her husband, the king.

More importantly, she made her supplications known to God, before she approached the king. This entitled her to a heavenly mandate and judgement from God, which she was able to exercise in the physical realm.

The king heeded to Esther's plea and replaced his first decree with a second decree. This second decree, replaced the first decree of destruction, with words of peace and truth, also for the generations to come. The power thereof, standing even to this very day.

"And he sent the letters unto all the Jews, to the hundred twenty and seven provinces of the kingdom of Ahasuerus, with words of peace and truth,
To confirm these days of Purim in their times appointed, according as Mordecai the Jew and Esther the queen had enjoined them, and as they had decreed for themselves and for their seed, the matters of the fastings and their cry.
And the decree of Esther confirmed these matters of Purim; and it was written in the book."

Esther 9:30-32

When the enemy holds a decree against you, it will be used against you in the Heavenly Courts until it is substituted by another. Once you repent for your sins and transgressions, the Blood of Christ will testify on your behalf, and a new decree will be released to replace the one that was in possession of the enemy.

It is wise for the children of God to commit to writing decrees inspired by the Holy Spirit. Decrees may be written for yourself, your family, your business, your church or whatever sphere of influence you have authority over.

The following is a copy of a decree that was written by the owner of a business:

Our Vision, Subsequent Mission and All-Embracing Decree

Foreword

This decree is intended to bring delight to my Saviour, as a confession, by a humble servant of God. It is not meant to be academic nor a religious record. Hopefully, by God's Grace, there is a soul somewhere that agrees, albeit in Spirit.

It is my firm believe that the essence of true conviction is a deep, overwhelming concern over what I am, and not what I have done. Holiness of life is far more important than holiness of doctrine. Furthermore, doing right is infinitely more important than merely talking about it.

Indeed, our troubles do not necessarily miraculously disappear once we dedicate our lives to God. However, we shall no doubt receive unshakeable faith to overcome all our afflictions and tribulations by the grace of God; and in so doing, exalt His Holy name.

While we shall surely have to endure storms in our lives that are possibly devastating, rest assured that we shall be victorious throughout, by our utter dependence on the Lord Almighty for our definite deliverance.

It is truly a sad misconception that our secular minds are polluted to such an extent that we vehemently believe our success is due to our own abilities and not by the grace of God alone. On the other hand, it is even worse to believe that the calamities one suffers are as a result of the wrath of God, rather than perpetrated by the enemy.

"Be careful for nothing; but in everything by prayer and supplication with thanksgiving let your requests be made known unto God.
And the peace of God, which passeth all understanding, shall keep your hearts and minds through Christ Jesus.
Finally, brethren, whatsoever things are true, whatsoever things are honest, whatsoever things are just, whatsoever things are pure, whatsoever things are lovely, whatsoever things are of good report; if there be any virtue, and if there be any praise, think on these things."

Philippians 4:6-8

Our Vision

I firmly believe that it is only when whatever we do, is done in His name, that God will do whatever we ask, in His name.

Neither I, *My Name, nor My Company Name* exist first and foremost due to the efforts, actions or abilities of any human agent.

By the grace of God, we are who and what we are. The main focus of our vision is to heed the calling of full-time ministry in business. By minister, we do not refer to the normal Sunday sermons, but rather to lead by example and actions.

We realize that God has explicitly called and anointed this company to bring about transformation to the marketplace.

The requirement to be a minister is not religious education; rather, it is the spiritual conditioning coming from *"having been with Jesus" (Acts 4:13).*

As ministers of God, marketplace children of the Lord, need to know that spiritual warfare is a central component of our daily routines, so likewise, we need to equip ourselves to be able to withstand the adversary's onslaught.

Company name want to play a vital part in establishing God's Kingdom on earth by actively participating, and by our leadership, so that the Great Commission will be fulfilled and cities transformed.

To be anointed for business is to be set aside by God for service in the marketplace. We want to use our position as a ministry vehicle to transform the marketplace, so that the gospel will be preached and heard by, everyone under our influence.

By ministering to people in secular institutions, the marketplace ceases to be a stronghold of the enemy, and is transformed spiritually.

"Now then we are ambassadors for Christ, as though God did beseech you by us: we pray you in Christ's stead, be ye reconciled to God"

2 Corinthians 5:20

Our Mission

A very wise and enlightened soul once said that we should always make an assertive effort not to judge our neighbours because they sin differently to yourselves. Praise God for revelatory knowledge!

God designed profit to serve for an honourable purpose. The fact that it can be abused, should not prevent us from appreciating and exercising its divine intention. In the business world the divine intent behind profit, is that it serves as the incentive that keeps business happening.

When business happens we are able to support, care and uplift less fortunate people, and in doing so, we fulfil one of God's greatest commandments, to love thy neighbour.

Bridging the gap between rich and poor people is essential for the realizing of the kingdom of God. Possessing a deep urge to want to help, we no doubt give God tremendous pleasure in glorifying his name by truly caring for one another.

However, due to our arrogance, our help is often limited to the social gaps that man created through ethnic, denominational, ministerial, gender, generational, and marketplace divisions.

We acknowledge that God created everything, and so do not deny any part of God's Creation by being party to any such social divide. May the Lord, God grant us absolute faith to withstand these most powerful forces of darkness.

We furthermore declare that our circumstances are gifts from God. We shall embrace the system to such an extent to hopefully improve by bringing the Kingdom to our workplace.

Our aim is to partner with the Kingdom of heaven and to keep standing on the following five pillars:

To honour the highest Authority of the Kingdom.
To be obedient to the highest Authority of the Kingdom.
To live a life of love.
To live a life of righteousness.
To live a life of servant-hood.

Servant-hood is the secret to rulership. Should anyone lack any one of these principles they will fail in their attempts at partnering with the Kingdom of heaven.

While we know that people will always experience limitations, the eternity of God's presence is boundless.

We remain infinitely grateful that God chose us for this mission.

"That ye might walk worthy of the Lord unto all pleasing, being fruitful in every good work and increasing in the knowledge of God."

Colossians 1:10

"But none of these things move me, neither count I my life dear unto myself, so that I might finish my course with joy, and the ministry, which I have received of the Lord Jesus, to testify the gospel of the Grace of God."

Acts 20:24

Our Decree

We hereby decree that God is the CEO of *Company name*, Jesus Christ is the Chairman of the board, the Holy Spirit is our legal and spiritual counsel, and the boardroom is our pulpit.

We are humbled, not to be overcome with feelings of guilt for not dedicating this company to the Creator since inception, as we acknowledge that thoughts of despair and guilt are riddled with fear and are not Holy.

We cannot be filled with the Holy Spirit and at the same time walk in fear. We agree that there is room for only one inside of us.

We believe in God's all – encompassing love and forgiveness. We believe that nothing belongs to us entirely, and everything ultimately belongs to God.

We are merely given opportunities to glorify His name through our actions. Our devotion will be reflected through our own free will.

We are prepared to stand alone in the circle that our Lord has drawn, to endure all the ridicule and mockery, even from those closest to us, whilst we prepare the ark in the desert, as the Lord has commanded.

May the Lord grant us the inner peace to forgive and bless those that persecute us. May we not forget that we shall never receive salvation from the Lord if we do not repent and forgive those that trespass against us.

We reject the deception that the marketplace is nonspiritual and that we are not ordained ministers in the marketplace.

We have already welcomed the Lord Jesus into our workplace for His perfect efficiency, and so willingly await His command.

We shall not fail.

Therefore, *Company name* stands for the sublime purpose of the Glory of God!

With passionate conviction, we also believe, that He who started the good work in us will complete it.

"Hast thou not known? hast thou not heard, that the everlasting God, the Lord, the Creator of the ends of the earth, fainteth not, neither is weary?
There is no searching of His understanding.
He giveth power to the faint; and to them that have no might He increaseth strength.
Even the youths shall faint and be weary, and the young men shall utterly fall:
But they that wait upon the Lord shall renew their strength; they shall mount up with wings as eagles; they shall run, and not be weary; and they shall walk, and not faint."

Isaiah 40 : 28 – 31

May we accept the Lord's mercy to endeavour to become fearless spiritreneurs and so bring about a change in the marketplace that resonates throughout the universe, and may the Almighty God whom we serve, one day utter the words, "Well done, good and faithful servant".

- Contracts

"And I will give unto thee the keys of the kingdom of heaven: and whatsoever thou shalt bind on earth shall be bound in heaven: and whatsoever thou shalt loose on earth shall be loosed in heaven."

Matthew 16:19

In the scripture above, Jesus is specifically referring to the binding and loosing of contracts. Any written or verbal contract, which you bind or loose on earth, is legally bound or loosed in heaven, and vice versa.

The following experience will reveal the power within contracts:

A few years ago, a woman in a terrible state of fear, phoned for help due to the prevalence of demonic manifestations in her home. Doors opened and shut, objects were moved around and the lights switched on and off by themselves.

On arriving at the property to assist in the matter, the Holy Spirit revealed that the woman's mother- in- law had signed a contract with Satan. This contract stipulated that every firstborn son would be dedicated to him, and in return she would receive wealth.
This binding contract gave the enemy the legal right to release familiar spirits upon the family in an attempt to kill their firstborn sons. By grace, this family were Born Again children of God, consequently they were under the protective blood of Christ.

Slyly, the enemy attempted to enforce fear upon them, in the hope that they would turn to occultism in their attempt to resolve this matter. Had they indeed attempted to resolve it through occultism, they would have opened a door that would likely have led to physical death.

As the family repented for the sins of their forefathers, the blood testified on their behalf and so the contract was annulled in heaven. The enemy's legal right was removed and the demonic spirits were ordered to leave the house, never to return.

- Covenants

"And I, behold, I establish my covenant with you, and with your seed after you;"

Genesis 9:9

A covenant exists where two or more parties are bound together through

an agreement, established either between men, man and God or man and Satan.
The best example of the perfect covenant is that of the Godhead; with God the Father, the Son and the Holy Spirit, standing in equal relation to One another, continuously displaying preference and honour towards one another.

Numerous biblical examples referring to various covenants are found throughout Scripture:

- In Genesis 15 and 16, God established a covenant with Abraham accompanied by the sign of circumcision.
- Abimelech and Isaac settled their dispute concerning land, entering into a binding covenant to henceforth live in peace (Gen. 26:26-31).
- Rebecca and Isaac as husband and wife.
- Pharaoh and Joseph as king and governor.
- There is Elijah and Elisha as mentor and student;
- Joash and Elijah as king and prophet;
- Joshua and Caleb as soldiers and colleagues.
- The friendship between David and Jonathan was bound by an oath.
- In addition, Peter and John stood within a covenant to be brethren within the Body of Christ.

"And it came to pass, when he had made an end of speaking unto Saul, that the soul of Jonathan was knit with the soul of David, and Jonathan loved him as his own soul."

1 Samuel 18:1

"Then Jonathan and David made a covenant, because he loved him as his own soul."
1 Samuel 18:3

A covenant is sealed by all the parties involved by vowing to fulfil certain responsibilities. These could include committing to love one another unconditionally, to pray for one another, and to support and encourage each other.

Covenants are ordained by God for His specific will and purpose to be executed on earth. These will extend to generations of the covenant bearers, and require continual sacrifice.

An oath is a pledge to assist one another to fulfil your respective callings, even if it entails sacrificing what is rightfully yours. The friendship of David and Jonathan is a prime example here.

In light of the nature of the proximity and purpose of covenants, these are likely to come under attack from the enemy; requiring the covenant bearers to resist severe oppression at times.
Stemming directly from God's personality, relationships are at the very core of all covenants. Since the Almighty is in essence a God of relationships, this truth testifies of Him as a God of love, Who desires a personal relationship with all mankind.

During a recent experience involving someone seeking help from another African country, the enemy presented a covenant as a legal right within the family's bloodlines.

A legal and binding covenant had been entered into between Satan and one of the family's forefathers. That forefather was a ruler who possessed vast tracts of land, but despite all of his wealth and influence, the family experienced numerous problems relating to rebellion and desire.

In a desperate attempt to resolve these family issues, he turned to what he thought were his ancestral spirits, making a covenant with them, not realising that he had entered into a binding covenant with Satan. The agreement stated that he would give the land he possessed to the ancestral spirits, provided they resolve his family issues.

The enemy is forever fiercely fighting to obtain territory, and so this agreement gave the enemy an extremely effective stronghold within that country. This covenant was disposed of so much power in the spiritual realm, that an oppressive portal was opened over that country.

The person seeking help, immediately repented for all the transgressions and abominations of the forefathers, and pleaded for Father God to destroy that evil covenant. The Lord heeded her supplications, destroyed the corrupt covenant, and entered into a new covenant between her and the generations to follow.

This new covenant sealed with the conquering and overruling power of the Blood of the Lamb shut the demonic portal over her country.

"Who are Israelites; to whom pertaineth the adoption, and the glory, and the covenants, and the giving of the law, and the service of God, and the promises;"

Romans 9:4

2

Fundamental Information on Jurisdictions

This chapter is divided into three parts:

- The Jurisdictional System in which there is a short summary explaining how God's entire creation is governed through His jurisdictional system.
- The authorities of the child of God, explaining how you receive jurisdiction by means of your authority.
- The Code of Law, by which the enemy is also bound to operate within specific jurisdictions.

The Jurisdictional System

"The LORD reigneth; let the earth rejoice; let the multitude of Isles be glad thereof.
Clouds and darkness are round about him: righteousness and judgement are the habitation of his throne.
A fire goeth before him, and burneth up his enemies round about.
His lightnings enlightened the world: the earth saw, and trembled.
The hills melted like wax at the presence of the LORD, at the presence of the Lord of the whole earth.
The heavens declare his righteousness, and all the people see his glory.
Confounded be all they that serve graven images, that boast themselves of idols: worship him, all ye gods. Zion heard, and was glad; and the daughters of Judah rejoiced because of thy judgements, O LORD."

Psalm 97:1-8

"But ye are come unto mount Sion, and unto the city of the living God, the heavenly Jerusalem, and to an innumerable company of angels,"

Hebrews 12:22

On earth, for justice to be done, a case needs to be presented in front of a court. The same applies in the Heavenly Courts.

We have the right, through Christ, to present cases within the various courts, utilising the various authorities. The right to present cases from that which is written in the scrolls is a resource that God made available to enable us to stand in victory and to support and protect us. This also gives the Judge over all of creation, the right to render judgement to bring justice on earth.

God rules the earth from His seat or throne of Government at Mount Sion, also known as the Heavenly Jerusalem. The Heavenly Jerusalem will come down from heaven to be established on the new earth after the Millennium, which is the 1000-year period that follows the second coming of Christ. After the Battle of Armageddon during the second coming of Christ, Jesus will establish His throne in Jerusalem, and rule the earth from there.

The enemy is in constant warfare, against anything involving God's government. This is the reason why the enemy is relentlessly attempting to destroy Jerusalem and Israel. In his view, the most effective way to hinder God from governing the earth, is to destroy His footstool.

"His seed shall endure for ever, and his throne as the sun before me."

Psalm 89:36

The Church forms an integral part of the jurisdictional system within the courts. All of creation is bound by these jurisdictions.

Before court proceedings commence, the Church of Christ needs to pray in order to release decrees and prophecies. This establishes justice on earth.

In some cases, it might be necessary to continually present our cases until such time that the court has obtained the right to render a verdict. This can be explained by means of the parable in *Luke chapter 18*.

Jesus told the parable about a woman, seeking the counsel of a judge who did not fear God nor regarded man. At first the judge did not relent to her supplications, but she pestered the judge beyond endurance, so he finally concluded that the only way he was going to enjoy peace was to grant her request. Jesus went on to say that God will avenge His own elect, who cry unto Him, day and night. Sometimes, like the woman in this parable, we need to press on, and continually supplicate our cases before the throne of our Righteous Judge.

The children of the light are locked in a perpetual territorial warfare with the enemy. For the Church to be victorious on the battlefield, we will need to understand how to operate strategically within the Heavenly Courts; to understand that these battles are fought, seated with Christ, in Heavenly Places. Places of authority and dominion.

We live in times where our knowledge of the spiritual realm is increased. This is part of the Lord's strategy, to lift the standard. As the attacks of the enemy become more powerful and fierce, so we will be equipped to never retreat and never surrender.

"But thou, O Daniel, shut up the words, and seal the book, even to the time of the end: many shall run to and fro, and knowledge shall be increased."

Daniel 12:4

As the Church, we can only present cases which are within our jurisdictional right. These jurisdictional rights are according to the authorities we have received from God, as His children, through Christ Jesus.

Authorities of the child of God

The Creator of the universe wants to release an outpouring of His Spirit on earth. Therefore, He needs His army of kings, apostles, prophets, evangelists, pastors and teachers to be ready to move in the power of the Holy Spirit. This is why we need to establish these heavenly offices, within all spheres of life.

"And hath made us kings and priests unto God and his Father; to him be glory and dominion for ever and ever. Amen."

Revelations 1:16

The more you grow in Christ and the more you bear the image of Christ, the more jurisdiction and authority will God entrust you with. He is calling His sons and daughters to be His ambassadors and faithfully continue the works of His Son, Jesus.

God wants to equip you to do even greater works, within all spheres of influence in these end times, to ensure that a lost and fallen world, is reclaimed for His Glory. For this vision to be successfully realised, you will need to know who you are, as a child of God, in Christ Jesus.

According to statistics, less than 5% of all Christians are familiar with their Godly callings.

Furthermore, around only 2% of the Body of Christ is involved in fulltime ministry for the sole reason that the rest of the Church are called to be involved in the other spheres of influence.

God has ordained that all spheres of influence on earth are arranged under the following mountains or divisions:

- The Ministry Mountain
- The Governance Mountain
- The Economy Mountain
- The Family Mountain
- The Media Mountain
- The Arts and Entertainment Mountain
- The Education Mountain

These mountains are discussed in more detail in chapter 3, but for the sake of the authorities of the child of God, it is imperative that the children of God rule in all these spheres. This will ensure that God's Kingdom is established and advanced on earth.

It is seriously problematic that the Body of Christ is unaware of their respective positions and callings to a large extent.

It is therefore imperative to pray for, and summon the prophets of the Lord with the anointing to reveal that which is written in the scrolls. This will unlock the ordained destinies, anointing and authorities of nations, businesses and individuals.

By destinies, anointing and authority, you need to understand the following:

- your destiny is your God-ordained calling
- your anointing is the ability you received from the Holy Spirit to execute specific tasks
- and your authority is the right to appear in certain heavenly courts and the extent to which you are permitted to gain territory through Christ.

"And he gave some apostles; an some, prophets; and some, evangelists; and some, pastors and teachers;
For the perfecting of the saints, for the work of the ministry, for the edifying of the body of Christ: Till we all come in the unity of the faith, and of the knowledge of the Son of God, unto a perfect man, unto the measure of the stature of the fullness of Christ:"

Ephesians 4:11-13

The Church of Christ needs to be adequately equipped and trained to serve within their priestly and kingly offices and therefore we need:

- Apostles building and establishing the Kingdom of God in all spheres of society.
- Prophets encouraging and edifying the children of God and His Church.
- Evangelists boldly sharing the gospel to all individuals, communities and nations.
- Shepherds feeding God's flock and supporting the children of God.
- Teachers, teaching the Word of God in power, in spirit and truth.
- Kings boldly advancing to secure territory and the silver and gold for the Kingdom of God.

While presenting a case on behalf of a businessman who was in Switzerland at the time, due to the urgency of the matter, the accuser immediately questioned our authority to present this case, once court was in session.

This illustrates how our identity and authority is also challenged. We had to know who we were in Christ, and had to understand the authority we had received to have the accusations successfully overruled.

Let us briefly explain the various positions within ministry.

- The Apostle

"Truly the signs of an apostle were wrought among you in all patience, in signs, and wonders, and mighty deeds."

2 Corinthians 12:12

The apostle stands in the privileged position as a forerunner for the Kingdom of God, in order to secure and prepare for what is to come. This anointing was specifically given to them by God and they will always be identified and announced by the true prophets of the Lord.

In this position one plays an active role by being a mighty pioneer in every plan and purpose of God. The apostle, therefore, needs to understand God's vision and purpose for the task at hand in order to establish it in fullness.

Apostles, together with prophets, have the authority to decree judgements released from the Heavenly Courts.

Despite the majority of apostles not being well known in the physical realm, they are certainly mighty men and woman of valour, and are honoured as true heroes in heaven.

God gave His Son as an example of how to serve with a humble heart, the same heart that His chosen apostles are to exhibit, by walking humbly among His people.

"Let this be in you, which was also in Christ Jesus:
Who, being in the form of God, thought it not robbery to be equal with God:
But made himself of no reputation, and took upon him the form of a servant, and was made in the likeness of men:"

Philippians 2:5-7

The main focus of an apostle is to take genuine interest in the building and restoring of each individual within the Body of Christ, and to be a mother or father figure towards the children of God.

The apostle Paul truly understood what it meant to mentor and father others, to encourage, train and equip them. Paul exponentially expanded the horizons of apostleship by not only fathering and mentoring individuals like Timothy and Philemon, but also entire congregations like the one in the book of Corinthians.

Apostles are called to lead the Church through the vision and foresight that God has given and also to help the people of the Lord to regain their focus on the main objective, when necessary. They spend their time developing and extending the plan and purpose at hand, and enthusiastically build on the platform of God's vision.

They are excellent in establishing churches, because they have an anointing and authority to represent groups of people, cities and nations within the Heavenly Courts. They are therefore keen and great advocates for the Kingdom of the Lord in the Spirit.

- The Prophet

"Yet the LORD testified against Israel, and against Judah, by all the prophets, and by all the seers, saying, Turn ye from your evil ways, and keep my commandments and my statutes, according to all the law which I commanded your fathers, and which I sent to you by my servants the prophets."

2 Kings 17:13

Prophets are tasked with voicing and revealing God's will and purpose, and so, are called to influence the people, communities, and nations. Prophets are commissioned to reach out to the child of God as well as to the rest of the world, by carrying the message that always focus directly on Jesus Christ.

They are sent with messages pertaining to exhortation, vision, direction, warnings, correction and judgement. They will also strengthen and guide rulers with wise counsel. A wise ruler will never alienate him or herself from the true prophets of the Lord.

Prophets encourage the children of God to remain faithful, and they resist evil onslaughts from within the Heavenly Courts. In the Heavenly Courts they also obtain judgements to receive the right to destroy demonic strongholds and structures, and teach others to do likewise.
The true prophets of the Lord need to heed to the call to take up their heavenly authorities and positions seated with Christ, so that earth may

be invaded by the Kingdom of Light.

Prophets who have been silenced, rejected, and wounded through persecution, are implored to listen attentively to what His Spirit is saying. They are called to return to their first love, to prophesy, to exude courage under fire, and to proclaim the Word of the Lord with boldness.

Prophets should not be deterred by the past as the times and seasons have changed. The time has come for the true prophets of the Almighty to rise and let their voices deliver God's messages and judgements, echoing to the farthest reaches of the spiritual.

This is the call of the Father for His eagles to rise up in power, might, spirit, truth and righteousness; to fearlessly deliver His judgements while all look towards the heavens as they hear the unmistakable sound of His eagles.

- The Evangelist

"And he said unto them, Go ye into all the world, and preach the gospel to every creature.
He that believeth and is baptized shall be saved; but he that believeth not shall be damned.
And these signs shall follow them that believe; In my name shall they cast out devils; they shall speak with new tongues;
They shall take up serpents; and if they drink any deadly thing, it shall not hurt them; they shall lay hands on the sick, and they shall recover."

Mark 16: 15-18

The evangelist stands in the key position to echo God's heartbeat for all souls for the heart of the Father is for all to be saved.

"For this is good and acceptable in the sight of God our Saviour;
Who will have all men to be saved, and to come unto the knowledge of the truth."

1 Timothy 2: 3-4

Although it is required of all God's children to share the gospel with others, the calling of the evangelist is more strategic, by nature, as the winning of souls is a unique authority for which they are particularly anointed. Winning souls may entail a few or even a multitude, depending on the field of specialisation and level of authority that God bestows.

Evangelists are blessed with the anointing to persuade average sinners as well as hardened backsliders that Jesus Christ is the way, the truth and the life. Provided they act within their jurisdictional right, they have the right to plead for the souls of individuals and nations within the Heavenly Courts.

Evangelists also obtain mandates empowering them to spread the gospel into the world.

This means that they literally receive the ability to bring the Kingdom of Light to the lost world of the kingdom of darkness, as they are first and foremost, fishers of men.

Innumerable evangelists have been sent out into the world to spread the gospel in places where mankind feared to tread. Therefore, being a truly dedicated evangelist, would require one to have boldness of heart, and for the gift of faith to be wholly activated by trusting God completely.

- The Pastor (Shepherd)

"Feed the flock of God which is among you, taking the oversight thereof, not by constraint, but willingly; not for filthy lucre, but of a ready mind;
Neither as being lords over God's heritage, but being ensamples to the flock.
And when the chief Shepherd shall appear, ye shall receive a crown of glory that fadeth not away."

1 Peter 5:2-4

Operating within the anointing and authority of a pastor is a most fulfilling experience, as it is usually very gratifying. Pastors are presented with the opportunity to engage with the flock of the Lord, to nurture and care for them, and protect them from false doctrine.

As a young boy, King David, the most well-known shepherd of all time, no doubt received shepherding training from his father and elder brothers. However, the moment he accepted his anointing and authority from the Lord in the position as His Shepherd, he started to receive the majority of his training from the Lord Himself, whilst herding and caring for the sheep on a daily basis.

The Word of God declares that the anointing of the Holy Spirit within us is more than sufficient to equip us regarding the authorities of the child of God.

"But the anointing which ye have received of him abideth in you, and ye need not that any man teach you: but as the same anointing teacheth you of all things, and is truth, and is no lie, and even as it hath taught you, ye shall abide in him."

1 John 2:27

It was the early days in David's life that played a significant role in laying down the Godly foundations he would need to safeguard and care for the nation, as King.
The analogy of the shepherd and his flock compared to that of the pastor and the congregation are very appropriate, bearing many similarities.

Like sheep, people need to be nurtured, protected, led, and raised to walk in the fullness of their purpose. Also, like sheep, people easily go astray without proper guidance. Backslidden individuals need to be approached gently by giving them a sense of belonging and purpose so that they willingly join the flock again. All lost souls need to hear the message of salvation, and an asserted effort needs to be made in order to integrate them into the Body of Christ.

The calling of a pastor is very dynamic, with tremendous variety, requiring one need to be willing and prepared to minister to God's entire flock.

Some pastors are called to shepherd individuals as Elders, while others are entrusted with ministries and even nations. Shepherds have the authority in the Heavenly Courts to represent those whom they were entrusted with. It is their duty to keep the Body of Christ together in unity, to plead for the protection of their people and to gather the ones who have gone astray.

- The Teacher

"And he came down to Capernaum, a city of Galilee, and taught them on the sabbath days. And they were astonished at his doctrine: for his word was with power."

Luke 4:31-32

An individual, ministry or business that is anointed with the mantle of a teacher, is called to bring the Body of Christ to spiritual maturity. The authority given to the office of a teacher enables him or her to teach and instruct others in the ways and principles of God and His Kingdom.

The teacher uses the Word of God to bring discernment and spiritual enlightenment to those who hear it and to be able to distinguish between what is true and what is false. He or she, therefore, also receives the authority to bring correction to false doctrine, teachings and principles within all spheres of influence.

Teachers have the God-given ability to interpret the Word of God correctly and relay it understandably to others. Through their anointed teaching ability, they endeavour to keep the Word of God relevant to whomever is listening.

The core foundation for the teachings and instructions for those called to serve in the office of a teacher is the Word of God. As such, the Word of God is the teacher's most significant instrument used to instruct, teach, correct and equip God's children.

"All scripture is given by inspiration of God, and is profitable for doctrine, for reproof, for correction, for instruction in righteousness: That the man of God may be perfect, throughly furnished unto all good works."

2 Timothy 3:16-17

The main objectives of the teachings, instructions, revelations, and corrections proclaimed by the teacher, are to empower and equip the Body of Christ with the true knowledge of God. They seek to teach pure Holy Spirit-inspired doctrine, diligently establishing a true

understanding of God and His ways to all they encounter.
Teachers bear a great responsibility within the Body of Christ and will be held accountable by God for the lives of all they encountered. God fearing teachers should testify of the truthfulness and the power within the Word they teach and profess.

"My brethren, be not many masters, knowing that we shall receive the greater condemnation."

James 3:1

Within their jurisdictional right, Teachers should take up authority, in the Heavenly Courts to release truth and Holy Spirit inspired doctrine, teachings and strategy to train and equip the Body of Christ. They should also plead for the Holy Spirit to be exposed over the generations to come, so that they may be susceptible to the ways of the Lord.

- The King

"By me kings reign, and princes decree justice."

Proverbs 8:15

Kings are the business-minded people anointed by God to function within the marketplace. They are more often than not, business owners, and are called to lead. As rulers, kings are called to reign over their kingdoms with mercy, righteousness, kindness, wisdom, biblical principles and the fear of the Lord.
They have the authority to possess land and to build; by which they expand and advance the Kingdom of God. They also receive the authority to establish decrees, and to co-operate with governors and prophets.

In order to operate within the Heavenly Courts, the authority a king would have, will depend on the nature of the business and their level of spiritual maturity.

Kings should understand that they are called to be Godly rulers of their communities and kingdoms and should reign as good stewards by caring for and serving the people.

Contrary to the norm, God did not entrust them with the anointing to control the wealth of the world, to empower themselves. They are indeed called to empower the Kingdom of God and will be held accountable for everything God has given them, as every good gift comes from the Father.

"Every good gift and every perfect gift is from above, and cometh down from the Father of lights, with whom is no variableness, neither shadow of turning."

James 1:17

In order to establish a specific business, a comprehensive example is given of the various navigations that were required within all the Heavenly Courts.

- Other Authorities

Much remains to be said about other authorities and anointing received from God. However, for the purposes of this book, we will only briefly touch on a few points here.

We are dressed in the spirit with garments and mantles according to our authorities and anointing, which we are to keep undefiled by sin, and pure through the redemptive power of the blood of the Lamb.

"Behold, I come as a thief. Blessed is he that watcheth, and keepeth his garments, lest he walk naked, and they see his shame."

Revelation 16:15

Some are dressed with garments of praise, victory, worship, salvation, joy, and perseverance; while others are dressed in the garments of a governor or royalty.

Some garments or mantles reflect a specific biblical anointing, for example the authority and anointing of Moses, David, Elijah, Esther, Gideon, Samuel, Paul, and many others. However, these authorities and anointing are all mere reflections of the true authority of Jesus Christ Himself.

We should have the motivation to be willing and prepared to go beyond the call of duty, to build on the foundations these biblical people have laid before us.

An excellent example in the Word, of one person receiving another's mantle, is that of Elijah and Elisha. This is also great proof of the authority associated with a mantle.

"And Elijah took his mantle, and wrapped it together, and smote the waters, and they were divided hither and thither, so that they two went over on dry ground.
And it came to pass, when they were gone over, that Elijah said unto Elisha, Ask what I shall do for thee, before I be taken away from thee. And Elisha said, I pray thee, let a double portion of thy spirit be upon me.
And he said, Thou hast asked a hard thing: nevertheless, if thou see me when I am

taken from thee, it shall be so unto thee; but if not, it shall not be so.
And it came to pass, as they still went on, and talked, that, behold, there appeared a chariot of fire, and horses of fire, and parted them both asunder; and Elijah went up by a whirlwind into heaven.
And Elisha saw it, and he cried, My father, my father, the chariot of Israel, and the horsemen thereof.
And he saw him no more: and he took hold of his own clothes, and rent them in two pieces.
He took up also the mantle of Elijah that fell from him, and went back, and stood by the bank of Jordan;"

2 Kings 2:8-13

Mantles are given to individuals or as a corporate authority to a specific ministry, business, community, or country. The various mantles dispose of different authorities in the Heavenly Courts.

In order to wear these mantles or garments with their rightfully intended purpose, one would need to know exactly who one is in Christ.

Using one's authority from a heavenly position will have a positive impact on the Body of Christ which goes beyond mere human comprehension.

The Code of Law

Depending on the circumstances, it is quite possible that one may find oneself in more or less the same spiritual battle continuously. This creates a long term problem that is extremely draining on the human body. We will become exhausted after numerous spiritual warfare's, following up on one another, especially if there is no lasting victory. The enemy, however, can carry on relentlessly, never growing tired.

After seeking God's counsel for a solution on the matter, we were instructed to establish a Code of Law for our kingdom (business). The purpose of this Code of Law is to create boundaries and to remove continuous legal right from the enemy to prevent engagements in the same spiritual warfare.

This Code of Law does not refer to the Mosaic laws of the Old Testament (by which the Israelites were guided on how to conduct themselves in the ways and will of the Lord) but refers to the laws of God by which the whole universe is regulated.

These laws have been revealed, albeit it probably in part, to us, by the Holy Spirit. Through scriptures ranging from the book of Genesis, all the way to Revelation. It is applicable to all of mankind and whether one truly serves the Creator is therefore irrelevant for these laws to apply.

The Code of Law of Our Kingdom

"This book of the law shall not depart out of thy mouth; but thou shalt meditate therein day and night, that thou mayest observe to do according to all that is written therein: for then thou shalt make thy way prosperous, and thou shall have good success".

Joshua 1:8

Foreword

The following Code of Law is in existence because we received a direct instruction to create such a Code for our kingdoms from the Lord God Almighty, and we are privileged to be obedient in spite of our insignificance.

May this Code of Law strengthen our kingdom through our utter faithfulness and adherence to these written words, and may we stand victorious by the grace of our God through His only Son, Jesus Christ, and the guidance of the Holy Spirit.

Furthermore, may these words persuade us to keep walking in the light of the liberty that our Lord Jesus Christ accomplished for us by being crucified for our sins, and may we never be steered toward the wrong path of rules and regulations that was brought upon us by legalism.

Our Code aims to strengthen our relationship with the Father, which is the only road to our eternal deliverance.

We as a people of God concur that although we were born in sin, we received the liberty not to sin, to choose, and therefore acknowledge that this Code of Law was written, and is upheld, as an anchor for our salvation. May we live holy by these words, for He is Holy.

"For all have sinned, and come short of the glory of God".

Romans 3:23a.

"For God hath not called us unto uncleanness but unto holiness".

1 Thessalonians 4:7

Declaration

"For this is the covenant that I will make with the house of Israel after those days, saith the Lord; I will put my laws into their mind, and write them in their hearts: and I will be to them a God, and they shall be to me a people:
And they shall not teach every man his neighbour, and every man his brother, saying, Know the Lord: for all shall know me, from the least to the greatest.
For I will be merciful to their unrighteousness and their sins and the iniquities will I

remember no more.

In that he saith, A new covenant, he hath made the first old. Now that which decayeth and waxeth old is ready to vanish away".

Hebrews 8:10-13

We hereby declare that every person that enters into this kingdom, through whatsoever means, shall do so under the covenant of *Hebrews 8:10-13*, and that the Law as described in this book will be put into each relevant parties' mind, as well as to be written on their hearts.
We also declare that every party entering this kingdom will be made known before the Lord, from the least to the greatest, and that the Lord will be merciful to their unrighteousness and sins.

May the Lord, through the power in the blood of Jesus Christ, no longer remember their iniquities, for this is a covenant that was established between this kingdom, it's appointed, and anointed Ruler, the great Creator of the universe, His only begotten Son, Jesus Christ and the only true Holy Spirit of God.

We furthermore declare that we heed to the call of ministry in business, family, and faith to bring about a transformation in the world to establish God's Kingdom on earth, and by doing so fulfil the Great Commission. We are indeed anointed for subservience to the Lord God, and have as such been set aside for service in our life's calling.

"Now then we are ambassadors for Christ, as though God did beseech you by us: we pray you in Christ's stead, be ye reconciled to God."

2 Corinthians 5:20

May the Lord grant us the courage to remain true to this Code of Law not merely for the authority it possesses on paper, but because it is eternally written in our spirits and therefore it is integral to who we are in Christ.

"For as much as ye are manifestly declared to be the epistle of Christ ministered by us, written not with ink, but with the spirit of the living God; not in tables of stone, but in fleshly tables of the heart".

2 Corinthians 3:3

Definitions

The following terms used throughout this book are defined below:

"Code" – a system of principles or rules

"Eternal" – having no beginning and no end time, lasting forever

"Foundation" – an underlying basis or principle

"Kingdom" – the spiritual reign or authority of God; while kingdom in lower-case form also refers to our spiritual city and business

"Law" – the system of rules regulating the actions of its members and defining correct procedure or behaviour

"Lord" – the name for God, Jesus, or the Holy Spirit; meaning that He is above all other things

"Mercy" – compassion or forgiveness shown towards someone to whom it is within one's power to punish or harm

"Ministry[1]" – the work or vocation of a minister of religion; the work in our kingdom, our business, our family

"Personal" – that which is used and implemented by an individual

"Universal" – relating to all people or things in the world; or in a particular group, applicable to all cases and having a universal effect

Foundational Laws

We hereby declare that our kingdom is built upon the foundation of the Father, the Son, and the Holy Spirit by which we will glorify the eternal Kingdom through our perseverance in the truth. Ours is also a kingdom that is ruled by righteousness, peace, and joy through our daily tower of strength, the Holy Spirit.

"Therefore whosoever heareth these sayings of mine, and doeth them, I will liken unto him like a wise man, which built his house upon a rock".

Matthew 7:24

"For other foundation can no man lay than that is laid, which is Jesus Christ".

1 Corinthians 3:11

"For the Kingdom of God is not meat and drink; but righteousness, and peace and joy in the Holy Ghost".

Romans 14:17

---

[1]The original Greek words most often translated as MINISTER/MINISTRY are the words DIAKONOS/DIAKONIA, meaning SERVANT/SERVICE

We also rejoice that this kingdom was founded and is built upon the following promises, declaring these to be an integral part of our foundation, and that these promises include the written as well as the spoken promises of Father God:

"God is not a man, that He should lie; neither the Son of man, that He should repent: hath He said, and shall He not do it? Or hath He spoken and shall He not make it good".

Numbers 23:19

"If ye abide in me, and My words abide in you, ye shall ask what ye will, and it shall be done unto you".

John 15:7

"But my God shall supply all your needs according to His riches in glory by Christ Jesus".

Philippians 4:19

"The Lord is my shepherd; I shall not want".

Psalm 23:1

"And, behold this day I am going the way of all the earth: and ye know in all your hearts and in all your souls, that not one thing hath failed of all the good things which the Lord your God spake concerning you; all are come to pass unto you, and not one thing hath failed thereof".

Joshua 23:14

Above all, we continuously hold to *Deuteronomy 28: 1-14 and Numbers 6: 22-26.*

Universal Laws

These are the laws that were determined by the Holy Trinity, and having been ordained since the foundation of the universe, by which the whole universe is governed by the Creator. These include the following:

- The Law of God

"This is the covenant that I will make with them after those days, saith the Lord, I will put My laws into their hearts, and in their minds will I write them;".

Hebrews 10:16

"But this we know that we love the children of God, when we love God, and keep His commandments. For this is the love of God, that we keep His commandments: and His commandments are not grievous".

1 John 5: 2-3

"Ye shall not add unto the Word which I command you, neither shall ye diminish ought from it, that ye may keep the commandments of the Lord your God which I command you".

Deuteronomy 4: 2

"For it is written, As I live, saith the Lord, every knee shall bow to me, and every tongue shall confess to God.
So then every one of us shall give account of himself to God.
Let us therefore not judge one another anymore: but judge this rather, that no man put a stumbling block or an occasion to fall in his brother's way".

Romans 14:11-13

"If My people, which are called by My name, shall humble themselves, and pray, and seek My face, and turn from their wicked ways; then will I hear from heaven, and will

forgive their sin, and will heal their land".

2 Chronicles 7:14

"Jesus saith unto him, I am the way, the truth, and the life: no man cometh unto the Father but by Me".

John 14:15

Through our obedient adherence and admission to the law of God we may receive God's blessing on our kingdoms by His grace.

"By the blessing of the upright the city is exalted: but it is overthrown by the mouth of the wicked".

Proverbs 11:11

"Righteousness exalteth a nation: but sin is a reproach to any people".

Proverbs 14:34

"At what instant shall I speak concerning a nation, and concerning a kingdom to pluck up, and to pull down, and to pull down, and to destroy it;
If that nation, against whom I have pronounced, turn from their evil, I will repent of the evil I thought to do unto them.
And at what instant I shall speak concerning a nation and concerning a kingdom, to build and to plant it; If it do evil in my sight, that it obey not my voice, then I will repent of the good, wherewith I said I would benefit them.

Jeremiah 18:7-10

"If so be they will hearken, and turn every man from his evil way, that I may repent Me of the evil, which I purpose to do unto them because of the evil of their doings".

Jeremiah 26:3

"Blessed is the nation whose God is the Lord, and the people whom He hath chosen

for His own inheritance".

Psalm 33:12

At the same time, we are also reminded by God of the consequences of our failure to obey His laws.

"Son of man, when the land sinneth against Me by trespassing grievously, then will I stretch out mine hand upon it, and will break the staff of the bread thereof, and will send famine upon it, and will cut off man and beast from it:"

Ezekiel 14:13

"Behold, I set before you this day a blessing and a curse;
A blessing, if ye obey the commandments of the Lord your God, which I command you this day:
And a curse, if ye will not obey the commandments of the Lord your God, but turn aside out of the way which I command you this day, to go after other gods, which ye have not known".

Deuteronomy 11: 26-28

- The Law of Christ

"Think not that I am come to destroy the law, or the prophets: I am not come to destroy, but to fulfil".

Matthew 5:17

"Bear ye one another's burdens, and so fulfil the law of Christ".

Galatians 6:2

"Let no debt remain outstanding, except the continuing debt to love one another, for he who loves his fellow man has fulfilled the law.
For this, Thou shalt not commit adultery, Thou shalt not kill, Thou shalt not steal,

Thou shalt not bear false witness, Thou shalt not covet, and if there be any other commandment, it is briefly comprehended in this saying, namely, Thou shalt love thy neighbour as thyself.
Love worketh no ill to his neighbour: love is the fulfilling of the law".

Romans 13:8-10

"A new commandment I give unto you, that ye love one another; as I have loved you, that ye also love one another".

John 13:34

We declare in the name of Jesus Christ and by the blood of the Lamb, that every client, employee, employer, business relationship, and partnership that exists with the blessing of the Lord shall not be broken in future, but will remain joined in harmony and until such time that God decides that the particular time or season has passed.

"What therefore God hath joined together, let no man put asunder".

Mark 10:9

We conclude and acknowledge the Law of Christ through the following scriptures:

"Ye have heard that it was said by them of old time, Thou shalt not kill; and whosoever shall kill, shall be in danger of the judgement:
But I say unto you, That whosoever is angry with his brother without a cause shall be in danger of the judgement: and whosoever shall say to his brother, Raca, shall be in danger of the council: but whosoever shall say, Thou fool, shall be in danger of hell fire".

Matthew 5:21-22

"Agree with thine adversary quickly, whiles thou art in the way with him; lest at any time the adversary deliver thee to the judge, and the judge deliver thee to the officer, and thou be cast into prison".

Matthew 5:25

"Ye have heard that it was said by them of old time, Thou shalt not commit adultery: But I say unto you, That whosoever looketh on a woman to lust after her hath committed adultery with her already in his heart.

And if thy right eye offend thee, pluck it out, and cast it from thee: for it is profitable for thee that one of thy members should perish, and not that thy whole body should be cast into hell.

And if thy right hand offend thee, cut it off, and cast it from thee: for it is profitable for thee that one of thy members should perish, and not thy whole body should be cast into hell".

Matthew 5:27-30

"Again, ye have heard that it hath been said by them of Old time, Thou shalt not forswear thyself, but shalt perform unto the Lord thine oaths:

But I say unto you, Swear not at all; neither by heaven; for it is God's throne:

Nor by the earth; for it is his footstool: neither by Jerusalem; for it is the city of the great King. Neither shalt thou swear by thy head, because thoucanst not make one hair white or black.

But let your communication be , Yea, yea; Nay, nay: for whatsoever is more than these cometh of evil."

Matthew 5:33-37

"Ye have heard that it hath been said , An eye for an eye, and a tooth for a tooth: But I say unto you, That ye resist not evil: but whosoever shall smite thee on thy right cheek, turn to him the other also."

Matthew 5:38-39

"And if any man will sue thee at the law , and take away thy coat, let him have thy cloke also."

Matthew 5:40

"And whosoever shall compel thee to go a mile, go with him twain."

Matthew 5:41

"Give to him that asketh thee, and from him that would borrow of thee turn not thou away"

Matthew 5:42

"Ye have heard that it hath been said, Thou shalt love thy neighbour, and hate thine enemy. But I say unto you, Love your enemies, bless them that curse you, do good to them that hate you, and pray for them which despitefully use you, and persecute you;
That ye may be the children of your Father which is in heaven: for he maketh his sun to rise on the evil and on the good, and sendeth rain on the just and on the unjust.
For if ye love them whichlove you, what reward have ye? do not even the publicans the same?
And if ye salute your brethren only, what do ye more than others?
do not even the publicans so?
Be ye therefore perfect, even as your Father which is in heaven is perfect."

Matthew 5:43-48

- The Law of the Spirit

"For the law of the Spirit of life in Christ Jesus hath made me free from the law of sin and death".

Romans 8:2

"For ye have not received the spirit of bondage again to fear; but ye have received the

Spirit of adoption, whereby we cry, Abba, Father".

Romans 8:15

"This I say then, Walk in the Spirit, and ye shall not fulfil the lust of the flesh. For the flesh lusteth against the Spirit, and the Spirit against the flesh: and these are contrary the one to the other: so that ye cannot do the things that ye would.
But if ye be led of the Spirit, ye are not under the law.
Now the works of the flesh are manifest, which are these; Adultery, fornication, uncleanness, lasciviousness, idolatry, witchcraft, hatred, variance, emulations, wrath, strife, seditions, heresies, envyings, murders, drunkenness, revellings, and such like: of the which I tell you before, as I have also told you in time past , that they which do such things shall not inherit the kingdom of God.
But the fruit of the Spirit is love, joy, peace, longsuffering, gentleness, goodness, faith, Meekness, temperance: against such there is no law. And they that are Christ's have crucified the flesh with the affections and lusts.
If we live in the Spirit, let us also walk in the Spirit.
Let us not be desirous of vain glory, provoking one another, envying one another".

Galatians 5:16-26

- The Law of Righteousness

We stand in the firm knowledge that we are not made righteous through good works, but only through the blood of Jesus Christ.

"What shall we say then? That the Gentiles, which followed not after righteousness, have attained to righteousness, even the righteousness which is of faith. But Israel, which followed after the law of righteousness, hath not attained to the law of righteousness".

Romans 9:30-31

"But now the righteousness of God without the law is manifested, being witnessed by

the law and the prophets;
Even the righteousness of God which is by faith of Jesus Christ unto all and upon all them that believe: for there is no difference:
For all have sinned, and come short of the glory of God;
Being justified freely by his grace through the redemption that is in Christ Jesus:
Whom God hath set forth to be a propitiation through faith in his blood, to declare his righteousness for the remission of sins that are past, through the forbearance of God;
To declare, I say, at this time his righteousness: that he might be just, and the justifier of him which believeth in Jesus".

Romans 3:21-26

"That the righteousness of the law might be fulfilled in us, who walk not after the flesh, but after the Spirit".

Romans 8:4

"For they being ignorant of God's righteousness, and going about to establish their own righteousness, have not submitted themselves unto the righteousness of God".

Romans 10:3

- The Law of Faith

It is ultimately through our faith in which we shall move mountains, subdue kingdoms, obtain His promises, and please Father God.

"Where is boasting then? It is excluded. By what law? of works? Nay: but by the law of faith.
Therefore, we conclude that a man is justified by faith without the deeds of the law".

Romans 3:27-28

"Now faith is the substance of things hoped for, the evidence of things not seen.

For by it the elders obtained a good report.
Through faith we understand that the worlds were framed by the word
things which are seen were not made of things which do appear".

"But without faith it is impossible to please him: for he that cometh to God must believe that he is, and that he is a rewarder of them that diligently seek him".

Hebrews 11:6

"And what shall I more say? for the time would fail me to tell of Gedeon, and of Barak, and of Samson, and of Jephthae; of David also, and Samuel, and of the prophets:
Who through faith subdued kingdoms, wrought righteousness, obtained promises, stopped the mouths of lions".

Hebrews 11:32-33

"Behold, his soul which is lifted up is not upright in him: but the just shall live by his faith".

Habakkuk 2:4

- The Law of Liberty

We are all free from captivity or restraint through the blood of the Lamb that was shed on the cross, so that we may have the choice to exercise our freedom in Christ.
"Now the Lord is that Spirit: and where the Spirit of the Lord is, there is liberty".

2 Corinthians 3:17

"But before faith came, we were kept under the law, shut up unto the faith which should afterwards be revealed.

Wherefore the law was our schoolmaster to bring us unto Christ, that we might be justified by faith. But after that faith is come, we are no longer under a schoolmaster For ye are all the children of God by faith in Christ Jesus".

Galatians 3:23-26

- The Law of Life

In life we are bound by the principle of sowing and reaping. Sowing is a choice and we therefore choose to sow good seeds of love, words of encouragement and truth. By making good decisions, we will sow seeds of finances, resources, and of time.

We hereby declare that we will sow and reap in the correct seasons; that our seeds will not be stolen; that our seed will fall on good soil, and that every good seed the enemy has stolen will be redeemed, and will grow in acceleration.
We declare that all bad seeds sown in this kingdom will be destroyed by the fire of the Holy Spirit, and that all bad seeds will not be rooted and therefore will not grow.

We also declare that all bad seeds sown which have already rooted, will be uprooted in the name of Jesus Christ, and that it will be replaced by the following:
Joy, peace, love, hope, faith, favour, mercy, provision, breakthrough, blessings, expansion of the kingdom by taking territory, obedience, and the presence of the Lord.

"Give, and it shall be given unto you; good measure, pressed down, and shaken together and running over, shall men give into your bosom. For with the same measure that ye mete withal it shall be measured to you again".

Luke 6:38

"Be not deceived; God is not mocked: for whatsoever a man soweth, that shall he also reap".

Galatians 6:7

We shall:

- obey God's Law, and the environment (land) around us will be blessed (Deuteronomy 28:4 & 8)
- bless Israel – and therefore we will be blessed (Genesis 12:3)
- stay obedient to God, and therefore His blessing shall come upon us (Deuteronomy 11:26 & 27; 28:2; Psalm 33:12; Proverbs 14:34)
- repent of sins and transgressions, and therefore keep God's hand of judgement from our kingdom (Jeremiah 18:8; 2 Chronicles 7:14)
- fight for justice, and we will be blessed *(Psalm 106:3; Isaiah 61:8)*
- confess our sin, and God will forgive us *(1 John 1:9)*
- be merciful and we will receive mercy in return *(Matthew 5:7)*
- stand in faith, and we shall move mountains *(Matthew 17:20)*
- first seek God's Kingdom and His righteousness, and God will supply our needs *(Luke 12:31; Philippians 4:19; Matthew 6:33)*
- follow Christ, and all things in our life will work together for our good *(Romans 8:28)*
- do good and lend to others, and our reward will be great *(Luke 6:35)*
- give and it will be given back to us in good measure (Luke 6:38)
- sacrifice for Christ's sake, and receive a hundred-fold in return *(Matthew 20:29)*

- do charitable deeds in secret, and we will be rewarded openly *(Matthew 6:4)*
- have a good spirit, wisdom, and a merry heart; and it will be medicine to our bodies *(Proverbs 17:22; Proverbs 18:14; 4.22)*

Personal Laws

We declare that these are the guidelines that we commit to conduct ourselves by, through the mercy and grace of the Father, the Son, and the ever-present guidance of the Holy Spirit.

- Live a life of love

"And walk in love, as Christ also hath loved us, and hath given Himself for us an offering and a sacrifice to God for a sweet smelling savour".

Ephesians 5:2

- Live a life of holiness

"I beseech you therefore, brethren, by the mercies of God, that ye present your bodies a living sacrifice, holy, acceptable unto God, which is your reasonable service.
And be not conformed to this world: but be ye transformed by the renewing of your mind, that ye may prove what is that good, and acceptable, and perfect will of God".

Romans 12:1- 2

"Blessed are the pure in heart: for they shall see God".

Matthew 5:8

"Because it is written, be ye holy; for I am holy".

1 Peter 1:16

- Live a life of honesty

"Dear children, let us not love with words or speech but with actions and in truth".

1 John 3:18

"To do what is right and just is more acceptable to the Lord than sacrifice".

Proverbs 21:2

- Live a life of servant hood

"Jesus answered him, It is written, You shall worship the Lord your God and serve Him only".

Luke 4:8

"Wherefore we receiving a kingdom which cannot be moved, let us have grace whereby we may serve God acceptably with reverence and Godly fear:"

Hebrews 12:28

- Live a life of glorification

"Let them give glory to the Lord and declare His praise in the coastlands".

Isaiah 42:12

"I will praise the name of God with song and magnify Him with thanksgiving".

Psalm 69:30

"I will give thanks to You, O Lord my God, with all my heart, and will glorify your name forever".

Psalm 86:12

- Live a life of obedience

"Do not merely listen to the Word, and so deceive yourselves. Do what it says".

James 1:22

"If ye love Me, keep My commandments".

John 14:15

- Live a life of humility

"And whosoever shall exhalt himself shall be abased; and he that shall humble himself, shall be exalted".

Matthew 23:12

"With all lowliness and meekness, with longsuffering, forbearing one another in love".

Ephesians 4:2

- Live a life of gratitude

"In everything give thanks: for this is the will of God in Christ Jesus concerning you".

1 Thessalonians 5:18

- Live a life of honour

"Honour all men. Love the brotherhood. Fear God. Honour the king".

1 Peter 2:17

"And no man taketh this honour unto himself, but he that is called of God".

Hebrews 5:4

- Live a life of giving

"Every man according as he purposeth in his heart, so let him give; not grudgingly or of necessity: for God loveth a cheerful giver".

2 Corinthians 9:7

"Withhold not good from them to whom it is due, when it is in the power of thine hand to do it".

Proverbs 3:27

"If a brother or sister be naked, and destitute of daily food,
And one of you say unto them, Depart in peace, be ye warmed and filled; notwithstanding ye give them not those things which are needful to the body; what doth it profit?
Even so faith, if it hath not works, is dead, being alone".

James 2:15-17

- Live a life of peace

"If it be possible, as much as lieth in you, live peaceably with all men".

Romans 12:18

"Blessed are the peacemakers: for they shall be called the children of God".

Matthew 5:9

- Live a life of forgiveness

"And be ye kind to one another, tender hearted, forgiving one another, even as God for Christ's sake hath forgiven you".

Ephesians 4:32

"For if ye forgive men their trespasses, your heavenly Father will also forgive you: But if ye forgive not men their trespasses, neither will your father forgive your trespasses".

Matthew 6:14-15

- Live a life of faithfulness

"He that is faithful in that which is least is faithful also in much: and he that is unjust in the least is unjust also in much".

Luke 16:10

"When thou vowest a vow unto God, defer not to pay it; for he hath no pleasure in fools: pay that which thou hast vowed".

Ecclesiastes 5:4

"But let your communication be, Yea, yea; Nay, nay: for whatsoever is more these cometh of evil".

Matthew 5:37

- Live a life of joy

"Let the saints be joyful in glory: let them sing aloud upon their beds.
Let the high praises of God be in their mouth, and a two-edged sword in their hand;"

Psalm 149:5-6

"Now the God of hope fill you with all joy and peace in believing, that ye may abound in hope, through the power of the Holy Ghost".

Romans 15:13

- Live a life of morality

"No man can serve two masters: for either he will hate the one, and love the other; or else he will hold to the one, and despise the other. Ye cannot serve God and mammon.

Matthew 6:24

"What? know ye not that your body is the temple of the Holy Ghost which is in you, which ye have of God, and ye are not your own?
For ye are bought with a price: therefore, glorify God in your body, and in your spirit, which are God's".

1 Corinthians 6:19-20

"And he said that which cometh out of the man, that defileth the man.
For from within, out of the heart of men, proceed evil thoughts, adulteries, fornications, murders, Thefts, covetousness, wickedness, deceit, lasciviousness, and evil eye, blasphemy, pride, foolishness: All these evil things come from within, and defile the man".

Mark 7:20-23

- Live a life of unity

"Fulfil ye my joy, that ye be likeminded, having the same love, being of one accord, of one mind".

Philippians 2:2

"That ye may with one mind and one mouth glorify God, even the Father of our Lord Jesus Christ".

Romans 15:6

"Finally, brethren, farewell. Be perfect, be of good comfort, be of one mind, live in peace; and the God of love and peace shall be with you".

2 Corinthians 13:11

- Live a life of compassion

"Thus saith the Lord; Execute ye judgement and righteousness, and deliver the spoiled out of the hand of the oppressor: and do no wrong, do no violence to the stranger, the fatherless, nor the widow, neither shed innocent blood in this place".

Jeremiah 22: 3

"Defend the poor and fatherless: do justice to the afflicted and needy.
Deliver the poor and needy: rid them out of the hand of the wicked".

Psalm 82:3-4

"And be ye kind one to another, tender hearted, forgiving one another, even as God for Christ's sake hath forgiven you".

Ephesians 4:32

"Bear ye one another's burdens, and so fulfil the law of Christ".

Galatians 6:2

"Finally, be ye all of one mind, having compassion one of another, love as brethren, be pitiful, be courteous:"

1 Peter 3:8

- Live a life of fairness

"Open thy mouth, judge righteously, and plead the cause of the poor and needy".

Proverbs 31:9

"Blessed are they that keep judgement, and he that doeth righteousness at all times".

Psalm 106:3

- Live a life of excellence

"He that hath knowledge spareth his words: and a man of understanding is of an excellent spirit".

Proverbs 17:27

"And whatsoever ye do, do it heartily, as to the Lord, and not unto men;"

Colossians 3:23

- Live a life of stewardship

"And the Lord said, Who then is that faithful and wise steward, whom his lord shall make ruler over his household, to give them their portion of meat in due season?"

Luke 12:42

"Moreover it is required in stewards, that a man be found faithful".

1 Corinthians 4:2

"Let no man seek his own, but every man another's wealth".

1 Corinthians 10:24

- Live a life of respect

"Let nothing be done through strife or vainglory; but in lowliness of mind let each esteem other better than themselves".

Philippians 2:3

"Honour all men. Love the brotherhood. Fear God. Honour the king".

1 Peter 2:17

- Live a life of Kingdom–mindedness

"Finally, brethren, whatsoever things are true, whatsoever things are honest, whatsoever things are just, whatsoever things are pure, whatsoever things are lovely, whatsoever things of good report; if any virtue, and if any praise, think on these things".

Philippians 4:8

"Set your affection on things above, not on things on the earth".

Colossians 3:2

- Law regarding fear

We shall never succumb to fear, however impossible or overwhelming our circumstances may seem; bearing in mind that fear is one of the four arrows by which our hearts are wounded.

"For God hath not given us the spirit of fear; but of power, and of love, and of a sound mind".

2 Timothy 1:7

"Fear thou not; for I am with thee: be not dismayed; for I am thy God: I will strengthen thee; yea, I will help thee; yea, I will uphold thee with the right hand of My righteousness".

Isaiah 41:10

"I sought the Lord, and He heard me, and He delivered me from all my fears".

Psalm 34:4

We shall only submit to the fear of God, the Son, and the Holy Spirit.

"The fear of the Lord is the beginning of wisdom: a good understanding have all they that do His commandments: His praise endureth forever.

Psalm 111:10

"The fear of the Lord tendeth to life: and he that hath it shall abide satisfied; he shall not be visited with evil".

Proverbs 19:23

"For ye have not received the spirit of bondage again to fear; but ye have received the Spirit of adoption, whereby we cry, Abba Father".

Romans 8:15

- Law regarding bribery

We shall under no circumstances be tempted by the temporary fruits of partaking in bribery.

"And thou shalt take no gift: for the gift blindeth the wise, and perverteth the words of the righteous"

Exodus 23:8

"For I know your manifold transgressions and your mighty sins: they afflict the just, they take a bribe, and they turn aside the poor in the gate from their right".

Amos 5:12

"For the congregation of hypocrites shall be desolate, and fire shall consume the tabernacles of bribery".

Job 15:34

- Law regarding confidentiality

We stand firm in our belief that we need to remain confidential with regard to our daily endeavours, and not to lend our ears out to ungodly news or information; but also being vigilant to avoid accusations of being shrouded in secrecy.

"A talebearer revealeth secrets: but he that is of a faithful spirit consealeth the matter".

Proverbs 11:13

We need to be led by the Spirit to attain the perfect balance between that which needs to be kept secret and that which needs be brought to the light.

We declare that whatsoever happens in this kingdom will be sealed and kept confidential in the spiritual dimension and that only God will approve of what may be revealed.

"He that dwelleth in the secret place of the most High shall abide under the shadow of the Almighty. He shall cover thee with His feathers, and under His wings shalt thou trust: His truth shall be thy shield and buckler".

Psalm 91: 1-4

- Law regarding family

We shall endeavour relentlessly to keep our family united in love through Christ. Understanding that this family is not only our immediate family, but also our family at the church, and the family we have at our place of work.

"But if any provide not for his own, and specially for those of his own house, he hath denied the faith, and is worse than an infidel".

1 Timothy 5:8

"Submitting yourselves one to another in the fear of God".

Ephesians 5:21

"For the promise is unto you, and to your children, and to all that are afar off, even as many as the Lord our God shall call".

Acts 2:39

"Be kindly affectioned one to another with brotherly love; in honour preferring one another;"

Romans 12:10

"As we have therefore opportunity, let us do good unto all men, especially unto them who are of the household of faith".

Galatians 6:10

- Law regarding leadership

We shall act as the true appointed and anointed leaders by the Holy Spirit and not by men according to the following Kingdom values:

"Neither as being lords over God's heritage, but being ensamples to the flock".

1 Peter 5:3

- to encourage at the right time when needed *(Judges 20:20)*
- to inspire by inspiration and not by manipulation *(2 Chronicles 35:2)*
- to influence others by our own example and way of living *(1 Corinthians 11:1)*
- to motivate with faith-filled words *(2 Samuel 11:25)*
- to lead in vision and purpose *(1 Chronicles 22:6)*

- to mobilize others to achieve certain goals and purposes *(Ephesians 4:12)*
- to activate followers in what God is calling them to do *(Colossians 4:17)*
- to convince people to follow God's vision *(Acts 18:28)*
- to correct and discipline followers *(Job 36:10)*
- to have a heart of a father and a mentor *(Job 29:16)*
- to remain teachable *(Proverbs 13:18)*
- to duplicate oneself by sharing one's mantle with others *(Matthew 28:19-20)*
- to be daring, bold, audacious, and fearless *(Joshua 1:9)*
- to be self–disciplined *(Proverbs 25:28)*
- to be compassionate *(Mark 6:34)*
- to make things happen *(James 1:22)*
- to have the right attitude *(Ephesians 4:31-32)*
- to have integrity *(Proverbs 10:9)*
- to have the desire to continually grow *(2 Peter 3:18)*
- to have the willingness to serve *(Ephesians 6:7)*
- to trust in others *(1 Corinthians 4:2)*
- to have the ability to communicate effectively *(Ephesians 4:29)*
- to be willing to confront problems *(1 Samuel 17:32-51)*
- to be self–controlled *(Galatians 5:23)*
- to be a peacemaker *(Romans 12:18)*
- to be dependent on God *(Proverbs 3:5-6)*
- to not be dependent on worldly approval and praise *(John 5:41)*
- to have initiative and be creative *(Exodus 35:31-32)*
- to be loyal and faithful *(1 Samuel 24:6-10)*
- to be humble *(Matthew 23:12)*
- to be clear, simple, and direct *(2 Corinthians 8:21)*

- to build relationships *(1 Corinthians 13:4-7)*
- to be able to empower others *(Romans 12:6-8)*
- to be able to serve *(Romans 12:9-13)*

"For the perfecting of the saints, for the work of the ministry, for the edifying of the body of Christ."

Ephesians 4:12

Above all, true Kingdom leaders need to have a close relationship with God, always.

- Law regarding materialism

We surrender and are vigilant of the fact that earthly possessions can be foolishly and wastefully utilised, abounding in self–indulgence and selfishness, whilst neglecting the needs of others. Living in the lap of luxury at the expense of one's neighbour in itself constitutes materialism, so we endeavour to distance ourselves from such behaviour.

"Lay not up for yourselves treasures upon earth, where moth and rust doth corrupt, and where thieves break through and steal:
But lay up for yourselves treasures in heaven, where neither moth nor rust doth corrupt, and where thieves do not break through nor steal:
For where your treasure is, there will your heart also be".

Matthew 6:19-21

By His infinite wisdom that was revealed to us by His Word, we know that resources can lead to the advancement of pride, which in turn leads one to become greedy and harbouring the need
to accumulate wealth for one's own sake.

We refrain from wrongful security in riches and ever acknowledge that all the silver and gold belongs to our Creator, also knowing that any wealth we possess is by His grace alone, and that we should be good stewards of His silver and gold.

"Go to now, ye rich men, weep and howl for your miseries that shall come upon you.
Your riches are corrupted, and your garments are motheaten.
Your gold and silver is cankered; and the rust of them shall be a witness against you, and shall eat your flesh as it were fire. Ye have heaped treasure together for the last days.
Behold, the hire of labourers who have reaped down your fields, which is of you kept back by fraud, crieth: and the cries of them which have reaped are entered into the ears of the Lord of sabaoth.
Ye have lived in pleasure on the earth, and been wanton; ye have nourished your hearts, as in a day of slaughter. Ye have condemned and killed the just; and he doth not resist you".

James 5:1-6

- Law regarding accountability

Although we submit to be accountable under any authority that God appoints above us, we shall ultimately be held accountable before the Holy Trinity for all our deeds, actions and words.

"So then every one of us shall give account of himself to God".

Romans 14:12

"But I say unto you, That every idle word that men shall speak, they shall give account thereof in the day of judgement.
For by thy words thou shalt be justified, and by thy words thou shalt be condemned".

Matthew 12:36-37

We declare that the rulers of our kingdom will abide in truth and in spirit by the council that was appointed by God through His grace. We shall remain faithful to such an appointed council for as long as they also remain faithful and true to the One.

"Where no counsel is, the people fall: but in the multitude of counsellors there is safety".

Proverbs 11: 14

"Without counsel purposes are disappointed: but in the multitude of counsellors they are established".

Proverbs 15:22

- Law regarding authority

We hereby declare that God is the source of all authority in the universe.

"Let every soul be subject unto the higher powers. For there is no power but of God: the powers that be are ordained of God".

Romans 13:1

"Obey them that have the rule over you, and submit yourselves: for they watch for your souls, as they that must give account, that they may do it with joy, and not with grief: for that is unprofitable for you".

Hebrews 13:17

We also declare that any degree of authority that a person has, was given by God insomuch as
that whoever resists authority, resists God Himself.

"Whosoever therefore resisteth the power, resisteth the ordinance of God: and they that resist shall receive to themselves damnation".

Romans 13:2

"And Jesus came and he spake unto them, saying, All power is given unto me in heaven and in earth".

Matthew 28:18

We solemnly submit ourselves to authority without which we are not able to receive authority; and adhere to the following basic rules of authority:

- The most effective way to express authority is with love, but not by manipulation, force, or domination.
- Do not exceed one's sphere of authority, as there are certain frontiers that should not be crossed.
- Everyone has a certain level of authority, as only Jesus has all the authority in heaven and earth.
- One needs to exercise authority responsibly, admitting when lines are crossed.
- We need to be held accountable within our positions of authority.
- We need to freely obey authority without rebellious urges.

"And if any man obey not our word by this epistle, note that man, and have no company with him, that he may be ashamed".

2 Thessalonians 3:14

"For to this end also did I write, that I might know the proof of you, whether ye be obedient in all things".

2 Corinthians 2:9

- Law regarding responsibility

"He said therefore, A certain nobleman went into a far country to receive for himself a kingdom, and to return.

And he called his ten servants, and delivered them ten pounds, and said unto them, Occupy till I come.

But his citizens hated him, and sent a message after him, saying, We will not have this man to reign over us.

And it came to pass, that when he was returned, having received the kingdom, then he commanded these servants to be called unto him, to whom he had given the money, that he might know how much every man had gained by trading.

Then came the first, saying, Lord, thy pound hath gained ten pounds.And he said unto him, Well, thou good servant: because thou hast been faithful in a very little, have thou authority over ten cities.

And the second came, saying, Lord, thy pound hath gained five pounds.

And he said likewise to him, Be thou also over five cities.

And another came, saying, Lord, behold, here is thy pound, which I have kept laid up in a napkin:

For I feared thee, because thou art an austere man: thou takest up that thou layedst not down, and reapest that thou didst not sow.

And he saith unto him, Out of thine own mouth will I judge thee, thou wicked servant. Thou knewest that I was an austere man, taking up that I laid not down, and reaping that I did not sow:

Wherefore then gavest not thou my money into the bank, that at my coming I might have required mine own with usury?

And he said unto them that stood by, Take from him the pound, and give it to him that hath ten pounds. (And they said unto him, Lord, he hath ten pounds.)

For I say unto you, That unto every one which hath shall be given; and from him that hath not, even that he hath shall be taken away from him.

But those mine enemies, which would not that I should reign over them, bring hither, and slay them before me".

Luke 19:12-27

As servants of Almighty God we do not only have a responsibility towards our fellow colleagues, but also to our community in general. The responsibilities to our colleagues are that we shall:

- Endeavour to relate to all colleagues, particularly those who serve in our ministry.
- Seek to serve our colleagues and their families with counsel, support, and personal assistance as the need may arise.
- Refuse to treat other colleagues as competitors, in order to maintain honour.
- Refrain from speaking disparagingly about colleagues.
- Uplift our fellow colleagues whenever possible.
- Treat colleagues with respect, fairness and courtesy.
- Respect any person of authority as being appointed by God.
- Be mindful in our conduct towards one another.
- Be honest and kind in our daily demeanour.
- Follow biblical procedure with regard to misconduct.

The responsibility that we wish to bear towards our community, is that we shall:

- Accept reasonable responsibility for community service.
- Support public morality in the community through honest witness and responsible social action.
- Obey the laws of my government unless they require my disobedience to the law of God.
- Practice Christian citizenship, without engaging in partisan politics

or activities that are unethical, unbiblical, or unwise and care for the needy and powerless.

- Live in peace and harmony with one another as far as possible.

"Wherefore the rather, brethren, give diligence to make your calling and election sure: for if ye do these things, ye shall never fall:"

1 Peter 1:10

- Decree of protection

We declare the words of *Psalm 91* for supernatural protection in our kingdom and rejoice, knowing that we are under the protection of the blood of the Lamb.

"He that dwelleth in the secret place of the most High shall abide under the shadow of the Almighty.

I will say of the LORD, He is my refuge and my fortress: my God; in him will I trust.

Surely he shall deliver thee from the snare of the fowler, and from the noisome pestilence.

He shall cover thee with his feathers, and under his wings shalt thou trust: his truth shall be thy shield and buckler.

Thou shalt not be afraid for the terror by night; nor for the arrow that flieth by day;

Nor for the pestilence that walketh in darkness; nor for the destruction that wasteth at noonday.

A thousand shall fall at thy side, and ten thousand at thy right hand; but it shall not come nigh thee.

Only with thine eyes shalt thou behold and see the reward of the wicked.

Because thou hast made the LORD, which is my refuge, even the most High, thy habitation;

There shall no evil befall thee, neither shall any plague come nigh thy dwelling.

For he shall give his angels charge over thee, to keep thee in all thy ways.

They shall bear thee up in their hands, lest thou dash thy foot against a stone.
Thou shalt tread upon the lion and adder: the young lion and the dragon shalt thou trample under feet.
Because he hath set his love upon me, therefore will I deliver him: I will set him on high, because he hath known my name.
He shall call upon me, and I will answer him: I will be with him in trouble; I will deliver him, and honour him.
With long life will I satisfy him, and show him my salvation".

Psalm 91

- Decree against unholy altars and portals

We declare hereby that any unholy altar that is erected in our kingdom will be summarily destroyed by the fire of the Holy Spirit; and that all demonic portals that are opened, be sealed by the blood of Jesus Christ.

Also we declare that the Godly spiritual portals and gateways shall never be sealed by the enemy; and therefore shall remain accessible for as long as it is ordained by the Father, the Son, and the Holy Spirit. Also, no holy altar that was erected in our kingdom may ever be brought down by the enemy.

"For our God is a consuming fire".

Hebrews 12:29

"Understand therefore this day, that the Lord thy God is he which goeth over before thee; as a consuming fire he shall destroy them, and he shall bring them down before thy face: so shalt thou drive them out, and destroy them quickly, as the Lord hath said unto thee".

Deuteronomy 9:3

"The LORD reigneth; let the earth rejoice; let the multitude of isles be glad thereof.
Clouds and darkness are round about him: righteousness and judgment are the habitation of his throne.
A fire goeth before him, and burneth up his enemies round about.
His lightnings enlightened the world: the earth saw, and trembled.
The hills melted like wax at the presence of the LORD, at the presence of the Lord of the whole earth.
The heavens declare his righteousness, and all the people see his glory.
Confounded be all they that serve graven images, that boast themselves of idols: worship him, all ye gods.
Zion heard, and was glad; and the daughters of Judah rejoiced because of *thy judgments, O LORD.*
For thou, LORD, art high above all the earth: thou art exalted far above all gods.
Ye that love the LORD, hate evil: he preserveth the souls of his saints; he delivereth them out of the hand of the wicked.
Light is sown for the righteous, and gladness for the upright in heart.
Rejoice in the LORD, ye righteous; and give thanks at the remembrance of his holiness".

Psalm 97

"We have an altar, whereof they have no right to eat which serve the tabernacle".

Hebrews 13:10

- Decree regarding times and seasons

We declare that our kingdom will move according to the times and seasons as determined by God; and that the enemy will not have any ability to influence our times and seasons. Any influence that the enemy might have instilled in the past, will henceforth be made powerless; and we declare God's original purpose and plan to arise evermore.

"And He changeth the times and the seasons: He removeth kings, and setteth up kings: He giveth wisdom unto the wise, and knowledge to them that know understanding:"

Daniel 2:21

"Nevertheless He left not himself without witness, in that He did good, and gave us rain from heaven, and fruitful seasons, filling our hearts with food and gladness".

Acts 14:17

- Decree against corrupt bloodlines

We hereby declare that any legal right that the enemy might have in our kingdom due to corrupt bloodlines be replaced with a blessing.

We pride ourselves in the blood of Jesus Christ and the promise that we shall receive blessings into the thousandth generation for them that love Him. Therefore, we hereby declare our love for the Father.

We also declare, in all humility, that when any accusation that the accuser bring against our kingdom due to corrupt bloodlines, our love for the Father be brought to remembrance, as well as the love that our ancestors harboured toward the Lord.

"And shewing mercy unto thousands of them that love Me, and keep my commandments".

Exodus 20:6

"And the Lord passed by before him, and proclaimed, The Lord, The Lord God, merciful and gracious, longsuffering, and abundant in goodness and truth,
Keeping mercy for thousands, forgiving iniquity and transgression and sin".

Exodus 34:6-7

We rejoice wholeheartedly in the promise that God spoke to Abraham, that through this promise all families on earth may be blessed.

"… and in thee shall all the families of the earth be blessed".

Genesis 12:3b.

- Decree of blessings to break curses

We hereby declare every curse, corrupt covenant, false contract, and evil decree, whether spoken or written, and erected against our kingdom, be destroyed by the blood of the Lamb and the consuming fire of the Holy Spirit.

We also declare that every curse, corrupt covenant, contract and decree that may exist be replaced by this written Code of Law of our kingdom and the following blessings and promises:

"Though shalt hide them in the secret of thy presence from the pride of man: thou shalt keep them secretly in a pavilion from the strife of tongues".

Psalm 31:20

"And it shall come to pass, that as ye were a curse among the heathen, O house of Judah, and house of Israel; so will I save you, and ye shall be a blessing: fear not, but let your hands be strong".

Zachariah 8:13

"And all nations shall call you blessed: for ye shall be a delightsome land, sayeth the Lord of hosts".

Malachi 3:12

"And seeing the multitudes, he went up into a mountain: and when he was set, his disciples came unto him:
And he opened his mouth, and taught them, saying,
Blessed are the poor in spirit: for theirs is the kingdom of heaven.
Blessed are they that mourn: for they shall be comforted.
Blessed are the meek: for they shall inherit the earth.
Blessed are they which do hunger and thirst after righteousness: for they shall be filled.
Blessed are the merciful: for they shall obtain mercy.
Blessed are the pure in heart: for they shall see God.
Blessed are the peacemakers: for they shall be called the children of God.
Blessed are they which are persecuted for righteousness' sake: for theirs is the kingdom of heaven.
Blessed are ye, when men shall revile you, and persecute you, and shall say all manner of evil against you falsely, for my sake.
Rejoice, and be exceeding glad: for great is your reward in heaven: for so persecuted they the prophets which were before you".

Matthew 5:1-12

"Blessed is he that considereth the poor: the LORD *will deliver him in time of trouble.*
The LORD *will preserve him, and keep him alive; and he shall be blessed upon the earth: and thou wilt not deliver him unto the will of his enemies.*
The LORD *will strengthen him upon the bed of languishing: thou wilt make all his bed in his sickness".*

Psalm 41:1-3

"The king shall joy in thy strength, O LORD*; and in thy salvation how greatly shall he rejoice!*
Thou hast given him his heart's desire, and hast not withholden the request of his lips. Selah.

For thou preventest him with the blessings of goodness: thou settest a crown of pure gold on his head.
He asked life of thee, and thou gavest it him, even length of days for ever and ever. His glory is great in thy salvation: honour and majesty hast thou laid upon him.
For thou hast made him most blessed for ever: thou hast made him exceeding glad with thy countenance.
For the king trusteth in the LORD, *and through the mercy of the most* High *he shall not be moved.*
Thine hand shall find out all thine enemies: thy right hand shall find out those that hate thee.
Thou shalt make them as a fiery oven in the time of thine anger: the LORD *shall swallow them up in his wrath, and the fire shall devour them.*
Their fruit shalt thou destroy from the earth, and their seed from among the children of men.
For they intended evil against thee: they imagined a mischievous device, which they are not able to perform.
Therefore, shalt thou make them turn their back, when thou shalt make ready thine arrows upon thy strings against the face of them.
Be thou exalted, LORD, *in thine own strength: so will we sing and praise thy power".*

Psalm 21

Mercy Laws

We hereby declare that whoever is indebted in any way whatsoever to our kingdom, may receive unconditional mercy, as mercy stands in authority against judgement.

May the example of our Creator lead us to show His mercy in the abundance that we have also received.

May we receive forbearance though the Holy Spirit to forgive one another as Christ forgave us; as Christ our Saviour, was not sent by the Father to judge, but rather to save us.

"Be ye therefore merciful, as your Father also is merciful".

Luke 6:36

"For he shall have judgement without mercy, that hath shown no mercy; and mercy rejoiceth against judgement".

James 2:13

"Blessed are the merciful; for they shall obtain mercy".

Matthew 5:7

"Forbearing one another, and forgiving one another, if any man have a quarrel against any; even as Christ forgave you, so also do ye".

Colossians 3:13

"For God sent not His Son into the world to condemn the world; but that the world through might be saved".

John 3:17

We also declare that should the enemy bring any accusation against any person in this kingdom that may result negatively upon us, we shall let the blood of Christ testify on our behalf through His spoken Word in *John 20:23*, and until such time that we are instructed by our Lord to act differently.

"Whosoever sins ye remit, they are remitted unto them; and whosoever sins ye retain, they are retained".

John 20:23

The written content of this Code of Law is not necessarily complete, but further revelation may be received through guidance of the Holy Spirit.

All kingdoms should stand for the sublime purpose of the glory of God. With passionate conviction, we firmly believe that He who started the good work in us, will also complete it.

May we receive the Lord's mercy in our endeavour to become fearless children; and so bring about a change in the world that resonates throughout the universe, that the God whom we serve, utter the words:

"Well done good and faithful servants".

Matthew 20:16

Above all, we remain grateful that God chose us for this earthly mission.

"And I heard a loud voice saying in heaven, Now is come salvation, and strength, and the Kingdom of our God, and the power of His Christ for the accuser of our brethren is cast down, which accused them before our God day and night.
And they overcame him by blood of the Lamb and the word of their testimony; and they loved not their lives unto the death".

Revelation 12:10-11

3

THE SEVEN HEAVENLY COURTS

It is our firm belief that the enemy is most certainly intensifying his onslaughts against mankind by his relentless attempts to take souls captive into eternal damnation. This is why God is raising up a standard by His Spirit, so that the children of Light may advance, in order to establish God's Kingdom on earth through power and rule.

Jesus Christ Himself, gave us the assurance that our knowledge would be multiplied during the last days.

The revelation knowledge we received regarding the Heavenly Courts needs to be applied by the child of God in order to be equipped to remain victorious, as it is God's will and purpose that we are properly prepared to resist and conquer the enemy.

The main objective of the Heavenly Courts is to give the child of God the ability to remove any legal right, of any kind, that may be in the enemy's possession; and in so doing, enable us to triumph over our adversary.

Each court is discussed in detail below, under the following headings: general information, experience, interpretation and relevance.

Please note that each narrative under the heading, experience, is directly quoted by Brigette.

The Court of Mercy and Grace

"Let us therefore come boldly unto the throne of grace, that we may obtain mercy, and find grace to help in time of need."

Hebrews 4:16

General information

- Any child of God may enter this Court.
- The Cloud of Witnesses together with a company of angels, are present, partaking in proceedings.
- Jesus is our Mediator in this Court.
- God, the Father, is the Judge.
- Satan or a cohort, are the accusers.
- This Court is held inside a building which is entered by passing through large doors.
- There is tremendous joy, peace and righteousness present.
- There is much laughter and spontaneous worship.
- Thousands upon thousands of people, worship and sing God's praise without any audible echo.
- There is always great jubilation whenever victory is obtained.

An experience

This Court is without a doubt the one most frequently visited. The following is an experience involving a community within South Africa:

"A married couple with a music school located in a very poor community, asked for heavenly mediation. The music school is used to reach out to children in the community as well as their parents. Being in a community where drug abuse is rife and most of the children are from broken homes where they were subjected to a life of fear and rejection.

As we entered into the Court of Mercy and Grace, the Cloud of Witnesses broke out in applause. My initial thoughts were that some great victory must have been accomplished, but the Holy Spirit corrected me, by informing me that the Cloud of Witnesses were honouring the authority of the couple as a spiritual mother and father.

God delights in us when we honour our mothers and fathers on earth; as every law God applies on earth as it is in heaven.

The scrolls were opened, revealing the destinies of the couple, their school, as well as every student and those still to become enrolled at the school. In addition, the scrolls containing the destiny of the community were opened.

As the couple supplicated their case for their school before the Lord, I became acutely aware that the heart of the Righteous Judge was for them to have an influence on the entire community, and not merely the school.

The accuser brought many accusations against the community and specifically claimed to have a legal right over the children, because the parents had rejected their seed and abandoned their offspring.

Unholy altars of bloodshed and corruption were erected in this community, as the enemy had control over it through Belial *(Judges 20:13)* and the force of Jezebel *(Revelation 2:20)*.

As the God-anointed spiritual parents, they had a right to represent the whole community. My spirit was stirred as I experienced the couple's love and passion for this community, as they started to repent in anguish over the accusations.

Inspired by the Holy Spirit, the woman started declaring that she and her husband accepted all the children, that they loved them as their own, and that the children were no longer orphans, nor rejected. As she was making this declaration, an angel of the Lord was writing down every word.

Immediately after she had finished, the angel proclaimed her decree over the community and upon hearing these words of acceptance, belonging and love, every human spirit in this community looked towards the heavens.

From amongst the Cloud of Witnesses there were people who were direct forefathers of some of the people in this community; and these also pleaded with God for their generations. Once the forefathers supplicated on behalf of their children, the saving and redeeming power of the blood of the Lamb testified, and gave the husband a legal right to break the curses.

The husband then started praying fervently against the bloodline curses of the community. Amazingly, he did not see nor hear anything inside the Court. However, he was guided perfectly by the Holy Spirit to do the right thing at the right moment.

Through times gone by, Holy Altars were erected by children of God who lived in the community. The living water flowing from every Holy

Altar in this community, testified against the unholy and corrupt altars which were destroyed by the consuming fire of the Holy Spirit.

"For our God is a consuming fire"

Hebrews 12:29

The Lord then asked the husband whether he was willing to accept the keys to the gates of this community, as an elder, and to stand in authority as the gatekeeper of this community. I was reminded that he who possesses the gates, possesses the city."

"That in blessing I will bless thee, and in multiplying I will multiply thy seed as the stars of heaven, and as the sand which is upon the sea shore; and thy seed shall possess the gates of his enemies."

Genesis 22:17

An interpretation

As the majority of the personal experiences related in chapters one and two are the interpretations of our visits to the Court of Mercy and Grace, no further explanation is necessary at this point.

The relevance

Whenever an individual, a family, or a business is struggling to achieve a breakthrough pertaining to a specific matter, this is the Court that needs to be visited.

If you have no doubt that what you are supplicating for, is within the will of the Father, but your breakthrough is still absent, the enemy may be in possession of a legal right that needs to be eliminated.

As a child of God, you have the freedom to boldly come to the Throne of Mercy and Grace with any matter that you expect a breakthrough with or may need to overcome in your life.

Those of you who possess national and international authority should frequent this Court often, in order to supplicate on behalf of your nation or even other parts of the world. However, it is of extreme importance that you obtain mandates, title deeds, and righteous judgements according to the jurisdictional authority entrusted to you by God.

Family bloodlines can be cleansed in this Court, and any legal rights the enemy may possess over a family, may be annulled here.

Contracts may be bound or loosed, heavenly decrees released, corrupt covenants destroyed, and righteous covenants may be established in this Court.

Permission can also be obtained from the Righteous Judge to be able to mediate and intercede in the other Courts according to the plans and purposes of the Lord. To receive mercy from the Father means in essence that souls can be saved, families protected, and territories may be gained.

Strategic plans for businesses, nations, and all spheres of influence can be released from this Court. In addition, one may obtain passes for protection against onslaughts for a specific period.

Fig. 1: The Court of Mercy and Grace

'he Court of the Council of Judges

"For I verily, as absent in body, but present in spirit, have judged already, as though I were present, concerning him that hath so done this deed,
In the name of our Lord Jesus Christ, when ye are gathered together, and my spirit, with the power of our Lord Jesus Christ,
To deliver such an one unto Satan for the destruction of the flesh, that the spirit may be saved in the day of the Lord Jesus."

1 Corinthians 5:3-5

General information

- In order to obtain permission to enter this Court, one has to have matured in the Lord, and hold the position of either an apostle, judge, elder or a king.
- Alternatively, one may also align oneself with any one of these authorities in order to gain access to this Court.
- This Court is held within a building.
- Jesus is seated on a throne to the right of the Father.
- Jesus Himself acts as a judge.
- The Council as well as the Cloud of Witnesses are present

An experience

"A friend of mine from South Africa, bearing the mantle of an apostle and the garment of a king, recently visited a church which he had been supporting in a neighbouring country.

The Lord revealed to him that there were two principalities of darkness present that were oppressing this country. The oppression caused widespread famine and poverty for such an extended time within this nation.

Inspired by the Holy Spirit, he entered into the Court of Mercy and Grace to repent on behalf of the people of this nation. He also pleaded that the destiny which is written in the book of this country would come to fulfilment.

After this, he was permitted to enter into the Court of the Council of Judges, where he was allowed to immediately deliver the verdict over the principalities that were oppressing the country.

"Thus saith the Lord of hosts; If thou wilt walk in my ways, and if thou wilt keep my charge, then thou shalt also judge my house, and shalt also keep my courts, and I will give thee places to walk among these that stand by."

Zechariah 3:7

On another occasion in this same Court, this time accompanied by a businessperson who was handicapped by an unrighteous partner, the Lord handed authority to this righteous businessperson to form part of His council as a judge.

"The king that faithfully judgeth the poor, his throne shall be established for ever."

Proverbs 29:17

Prior to our visit to this Court, the unrighteous partner had received ample warning from the Lord, to repent of his iniquities. The urgency of this matter also suddenly required attention when a key person supporting the unrighteous partner in the business, started openly practicing witchcraft.

The spirits of both the unrighteous partner as well as the person practicing witchcraft were summoned before this Council. The forces driving them, Jezebel and Mammon, were also summoned to appear; and a righteous verdict was established and delivered upon them all.

Up until that point in time, the real test for the righteous businessperson was whether he would gain victory in the physical realm over the works of Mammon and Jezebel.

The conclusion made on that day in this Court, was that victory had indeed been obtained by him over the works of both Jezebel and Mammon. A few weeks later, the righteous businessperson parted ways with his unrighteous partner for good."

An interpretation

For a better understanding of the Council of Judges let us first interpret the Council within both the physical and the spiritual realms, referred to by Jesus, in Matthew chapter five.

"Ye have heard that it was said by them of old time, Thou shalt not kill; and whosoever shall kill be in danger of the judgement:
But I say unto you, That whosoever is angry with his brother without a cause shall be in danger of the judgement: and whosoever shall say to his brother, Raca, shall be in danger of the council: but whosoever shall say, Thou fool, shall be in danger of hell fire."

Matthew 5:21-22

- The physical realm

According to "Ellicott's Commentary" this council is referred to as the great Court of the Sanhedrin. The Sanhedrin consisted of, either seventy, or seventy-two members, with a president and vice-president in leadership positions. These members were chosen from the twenty-four priests, with the rest of the forty-six or forty-eight members being chosen from among the elders or the scribes. Exactly what the process entailed by which the members were chosen, is not known.

In much the same manner as the Areopagus in Athens, they took cognisance of blasphemy and other similar offences; and their prerogative was that they could authorize death by stoning. Cases in point being that of our Lord Jesus Christ in *Matthew 26:65* and that of Stephen in *Acts 6:13.*

The Sanhedrin had its origin in the Council of the Seventy Elders founded by Moses.

"And the LORD said unto Moses, Gather unto me seventy men of the elders of Israel, whom thou knowest to be elders of the people, and officers over them; and bring them unto the tabernacle of the congregation, that they may stand there with thee."

Numbers 11:16

This first Sanhedrin consisted of seventy-one members, Moses included. As members within the Sanhedrin passed on, or otherwise became unfit for service, new members underwent Semicha ordination. These ordinations remained unbroken, from Moses to Joshua, to the elders, the prophets, the Great Assembly, to the sages of the Sanhedrin. (www.thesanhedrin.org)

One of the lessons we are to learn from Jesus's teaching in *Matthew 5:21-22* is that to scorn the image of God, in man, is to dishonour God Himself. Therefore, we cannot truly fear God, lest we honour all men.

"Honour all men. Love the brotherhood. Fear God. Honour the king."

1 Peter 2:17

As children of God, the respect we have for humanity, must extend, even to those who have provoked us the most. Remembering that provoking your brethren has consequences in the unseen spiritual world.

- The Spiritual Realm

From biblical times, the Sanhedrin was a reflection of the Council of Judges, operating within the Heavenly Court in the spiritual realm.

Together with the Supreme Jude, those who have matured in both mercy and righteousness are anointed to stand in authority, and serve as judges within this Court.

They have received authority to judge the principalities and rulers of darkness. The enemy needs to abide by the Law of God as well, and whenever the forces of darkness infringe their jurisdictional rights, they are summoned to appear and be dealt with in this Court.

The same principle applies when anyone violates the above-mentioned Law of Christ. Once summoned to this Court, those forming part of the Council of Judges will then partake in the Court proceedings.

Thankfully, through the Lord's unfathomable mercy and grace, we are always given ample opportunity to repent, before being summoned to appear before this Council.

Despite their obliviousness of the spiritual realm, most people will in any event be unaware of being summoned to appear in front of the Council of Judges. However, they will surely be aware that the Holy Spirit prompted them to repentance in the physical realm.

"And said to the judges, Take heed what ye do: for ye judge not for man, but for the LORD, who is with you in judgement.
Wherefore now let the fear of the LORD be upon you; take heed and do it: for there is no iniquity with the LORD our God, nor respect of persons, nor taking gifts.
Moreover in Jerusalem did Jehoshaphat set of the Levites, and of the priests, and of the chief of the fathers of Israel, for the judgement of the LORD, and for the controversies, when they returned to Jerusalem.
And he charged them, saying, Thus shall ye do in the fear of the LORD, faithfully, and with a perfect heart."

2 Chronicles 19:6-9

The relevance

Anyone standing in authority as judge should take up their seats in this Council to ensure that justice is rendered in perfect mercy and righteousness, so that His sovereign will may be done, and that the whole world unequivocally knows, that Almighty God, rules.

"This matter is by the decree of the watchers, and the demand by the word of the holy ones: to the intent that the living may know that the most High ruleth in the kingdom of men, and giveth it to whomsoever he will, and setteth up over it the basest of men."

Daniel 4:1

Fig. 2: The Court of the Council of Judges

The Parliamentary Court

"For unto us a child is born, unto us a son is given: and the government shall be upon his shoulder: and his name shall be called Wonderful, Counsellor, The mighty God, The everlasting Father, The Prince of Peace.
Of the increase of his government and peace there shall be no end, upon the throne of David, and upon his kingdom, to order it, and to establish it with judgement and with justice from henceforth even for ever.
The zeal of the LORD of hosts will perform this."
Isaiah 9:6-7

General information

- This Court is housed inside a building.
- In order to enter, you are required to stand in either a provincial or national governmental position.
- The children of God in the apostolic or prophetic authority may also gain access to this Court.
- Businesses conducting business with governments will receive authority to enter.
- Those representing the Kingdom of Light are seated to the right of the Father, and this position indicates favour.
- Those representing the kingdom of darkness are seated to the left of the Father, and this position indicates judgement.
- Jesus Christ is seated on a throne to the right of the Father.
- Jesus operates from within His authority as Ruler, Shepherd, and Counsellor over all governments.

An experience

“I assisted a businessperson who had an issue with the title deeds to his building.

The building itself had been erected on two separate stands. The one was registered in the name of the municipality (local government) and the other was registered in the name of Gautrans, representing the Department of Transport and Public Works.

This issue surrounding the stands had major bond implications with the bank. In the physical realm, Gautrans needed to provide the local municipality with a letter of consent, whereby the stand registered in their name would be incorporated with the stand registered in the name of the local government.

We commenced proceedings in the Heavenly Courts by entering the Court of Mercy and Grace, in order to remove any legal right, the enemy may have been in possession of. As such, we enquired of the Righteous Judge, regarding the foundations of the business, the clients, the employees, as well as the family involved, specifically, focussing on potentially corrupted bloodlines.

It is worthwhile to note, that these are the basic steps to commence with when starting an intercession for any business.

After removing all legal right in the enemy’s possession, the Lord granted us permission to enter the Parliamentary Court to resolve the issue pertaining to the stands.

Because judgement had already been rendered in the Court of Mercy and Grace, all that was still required was for someone representing God's Kingdom in the Parliamentary Court, to stand in agreement with our request. Where two or three are in agreement, so it will be.

Indeed, someone representing God's Kingdom rose to the occasion and declared that she was in agreement with our request, because she knew that this business bore good fruit. The Lord then released the correct title deeds to the property in the spiritual realm.

Two days after our visit to the Parliamentary Court, the requested letter of consent was obtained, and all matters were resolved. Needless to say, this businessperson's bond was also approved and registered accordingly."

An interpretation

A government is the system by which a state or community is controlled. Furthermore, the concepts of the state and the government may be used synonymously to refer to the person or group of people exercising authority over a politically organised territory.

Government is the means by which state policy is enforced, as well as the mechanism for determining the policy of a country or state. A form of government, or form of state governance, refers to the set of political systems and institutions that make up the organisation of a specific government

"Submit yourselves to every ordinance of man for the Lord's sake: whether it be to the king, as supreme; Or unto governors, as unto them that are sent by him for the

punishment of evildoers, and for the praise of them that do well."

1 Peter 2:13-14

All governments are subject to the rule of Christ and they are supposed to serve their respective peoples to the best of their abilities. Not through fear, but excellence.

Earthly parliaments are a reflection of the Parliamentary Court. Those who stand in the required position of authority will have a seat in this Heavenly Parliament and will either represent the Kingdom of Light or the kingdom of darkness.

The enemy often gains territory within a city or country, purely because the children of God are not seated within the Heavenly Parliament and are subsequently usurped by the evildoers.

According to the ordinances of God, the following are descriptions of the various types of governments. Although this will also apply to the International Court, you would need to possess international authority as well.

- Heavenly Government

Every child of God, who has taken up his or her positions and callings and endured for the sake of the Kingdom, will rule with Christ. Those who stood within governmental authority on earth will stand in governmental authority in heaven.

"I Daniel was grieved in my spirit in the midst of my body, and the visions of my head troubled me. I came near unto one of them that stood by, and asked him the truth of

all this. So he told me, and made me know the interpretation of the things.
These great beasts, which are four, are four kings, which shall arise out of the earth.
But the saints of the most High shall take the kingdom, and possess the kingdom for ever, even for ever and ever."

Daniel 7:15-18

"Therefore I endure all things for the elect's sakes, that they may also obtain the salvation which is in Christ Jesus with eternal glory.
It is a faithful saying: For if we be dead with him, we shall also live with him:
If we suffer, we shall also reign with him: if we deny him, he also will deny us:"

2 Timothy 2:10-12

- Ecclesiastical Governments

Apostles and elders are called to proclaim decrees over governments, cities, nations and continents.

Those within the Body of Christ, who stand in authority on the Governance Mountain, whether a prophet, apostle, governor, or businessperson, are called to stand for righteousness and the sovereign will of God to be done; to resist evil, and to establish God's government on earth.

The Apostles of the Lord need to take up their authority on the Governance Mountain to build Godly structure within governments, and to uproot and destroy evil structures.

The prophets should be God's voice to governments and rulers, and should release and prophecy God's judgements over governments.

"And as they went through the cities, they delivered them the decrees for to keep, that were ordained of the apostles and elders which were at Jerusalem."

Acts 16:4

- Kings, Princes and Rulers of the World

These rulers are appointed by the Lord to establish stability in the land through justice, and to rule righteously over their peoples, in the fear of the Lord. A throne or seat in governance is obtained through righteousness, and therefore it is an abomination in the eyes of the Lord for rulers to commit acts of wickedness.

"The king by judgment establisheth the land: but he that receiveth gifts overthroweth it."

Proverbs 29:4

- Provincial Governments

"Now in the fifteenth year of the reign of Tiberius Caesar, Pontius Pilate being governor of Judaea, and Herod being tetrarch of Galilee, and his brother Philip tetrarch of Ituraea and of the region of Trachonitis, and Lysanias the tetrarch of Abilene,

Annas and Caiaphas being the high priests, the word of God came unto John the son of Zacharias in the wilderness."

Luke 3:1-2

- Corrupt Governments

Those in a position of authority and who misuse their positions for evildoing, will surely be held accountable. The righteous will prevail against the dark forces, while the unrighteous will be cut off.

"And I said, Hear, I pray you, O heads of Jacob, and ye princes of the house of Israel; Is it not for you to know judgment?

Who hate the good, and love the evil; who pluck off their skin from off them, and their flesh from off their bones;

Who also eat the flesh of my people, and flay their skin from off them; and they break their bones, and chop them in pieces, as for the pot, and as flesh within the caldron.

Then shall they cry unto the LORD, but he will not hear them: he will even hide his face from them at that time, as they have behaved themselves ill in their doings.

Thus saith the LORD concerning the prophets that make my people err, that bite with their teeth, and cry, Peace; and he that putteth not into their mouths, they even prepare war against him.

Therefore night shall be unto you, that ye shall not have a vision; and it shall be dark unto you, that ye shall not divine; and the sun shall go down over the prophets, and the day shall be dark over them.

Then shall the seers be ashamed, and the diviners confounded: yea, they shall all cover their lips; for there is no answer of God.

But truly I am full of power by the spirit of the LORD, and of judgment, and of might, to declare unto Jacob his transgression, and to Israel his sin.

Hear this, I pray you, ye heads of the house of Jacob, and princes of the house of Israel, that abhor judgment, and pervert all equity."

Micah 3:1-3

The relevance

Those representing God's Kingdom should use their authority within this Court, to obtain righteous judgments, and to uproot evil systems and structures within governments. This Court should also be utilized to establish Godly government within a nation or province.

Business-people involved in dealings with governments also should

also make use of this Court to bind righteous contracts, and to receive authority to obtain territory.
When righteous business-people become aware of corrupt conduct within government, they should oppose this behaviour in the Parliamentary Court, by proclaiming justice and truth through the Word of God.

God's righteous should also oppose unrighteous decisions made by governments regarding the educational, media, economic and other spheres of influence. They should plead for righteousness to triumph, and decree scripture that speaks against all evil.

Fig. 3: The Parliamentary Court

The Court of Times and Seasons

In order to comprehend the Court of Times and Seasons it will be wise to get an understanding of the times and seasons through the ages of God first.

As with everything else in the universe, in order to comprehend the greatness of God and the universal plan that He has meticulously and painstakingly designed for us mere sinners, we need to try and grasp, that God also created time, and subsequently seasons came to pass.

It is almost unimaginable to think that the Creator of the universe would go through so much trouble and effort, to reveal His ultimate will, by rendering us as sinners, a chance to experience eternal peace and joy in His Almighty presence, by being in a constantly evolving personal relationship with the Holy Trinity.

Everything in the universe known to man and even that which is still unknown exists to glorify the Father, the Son and the Holy Spirit. Our constant attempts to seek His presence will inevitably reveal His incomprehensible redemptive mercies by which we, who were born in sin, may also receive salvation.
God regulates and has planned everything according to His ordained times and seasons. It is therefore imperative that we understand the times we live in if we want to understand what God is going to do.

For if we do not understand the times, as well as what God is doing, we would not know what to do. Being in uncertainty gives the enemy leverage that we simply cannot afford. To walk in complete surrender and trust in the ways of the Lord is at the worst of times an arduous, trying journey and the best of times a journey with rewards beyond human comprehension. This is the reason why God, through His mercy and grace, designed specific times and seasons for each and every individual.

To masterfully equip us to be able to remain standing, growing and advancing, surrounded by His all-encompassing love, so that we may take up our individual callings to ultimately achieve His will and purpose for us.

"To every thing there is a season, and a time to every purpose under the heaven:
A time to be born, and a time to die; a time to plant, and a time to pluck up that which is planted;
A time to kill, and a time to heal; a time to break down and a time to build up;
A time to weep, and a time to laugh; a time to mourn and a time to dance;
A time to cast away stones, and a time to gather stones together; a time to embrace, and a time to refrain from embracing;
A time to get, and a time to lose; a time to keep, and a time to cast away;
A time to rend, and a time to sew; a time to keep silence, and a time to speak;
A time to love, and a time to hate; a time of war, and a time of peace."

Ecclesiastes 3:1-8

Before we allow ourselves the possibly feeble attempt of grasping God's times and seasons it would be appropriate to look at the origination of the different words.

The meaning and origination of the words: Times and Seasons

"And He changeth the times and the seasons: He removeth kings, and setteth up kings: He giveth wisdom unto the wise, and knowledge to them that know understanding."

Daniel 2:21

The following is an extract from the "Daily Bible Study" by Wayne Blank:

As a noun the word time is defined as: "the indefinite continued progress of existence and events in the past, present and future regarded as a whole and a point of time as measured in hours and minutes past midnight or noon."

As a verb the word time is defined as a: "plan, schedule or arrangement when (something) should happen or be done."

The English word *"time"* originated from the same Anglo-Saxon root word as the English word *"tide"* (the periodic rise and fall of the sea level under the gravitational pull of the moon).

The Holy Scriptures translate the English word "time" or "times" from a number of Hebrew and Greek words. As is often the case, translations commonly use a "one meaning fits all" word for a surprising number of words that were originally written with an also surprising variety of literal meanings.

The following are a few examples of Hebrew words translated as "time" or "times":

- the Hebrew word pronounced *yome*, which means to be warm, used to refer to the time between sunrise and sunset
- the Hebrew word pronounced *ayth*, which means now or when
- the Hebrew word pronounced *tekh-il-law*, which means to begin
- the Hebrew word pronounced *mow-ad-dawh*, which means appointment or decided time
- the Hebrew word pronounced *id-dawn*, which means an appointed length of time

Here are several examples of Greek words translated as "time" or "times":

- the Greek word pronounced *ep-pee*, which means an epoch
- the Greek word *chronos*, which means the order or arrangement of events
- the Greek word pronounced *may-pot-eh*, which means not ever
- the Greek word pronounced *tote-eh*, which means then or at that time
- the Greek word pronounced *kairos,* which means the proper time

For the purposes of this writing we shall only look at the definition of the word season as a noun: "each of the four divisions of the year (spring, summer, autumn and winter) marked by particular weather patterns and daylight hours, resulting from the earth's changing position with regard to the sun."

The word "season" originated from a different Old English word "seson", which meant a time to sow.
The following are some examples of Hebrew words translated as "season" or "seasons":

- the Hebrew word pronounced *maw-lawkh*, which means to wear away
- the Hebrew word pronounced *ayth*, which means now or when but was used to refer to short "times" or long "seasons.

Greek words translated as "season" or "seasons", include the following examples:

- the Greek word pronounced *kah-hee-ros*, which means the proper time
- the Greek word pronounced *ar-too-oh*, which means to prepare

or mature

- the Greek word pronounced *ak-ah-ee-roce*, which means out of season

With the above in mind it is easy to see how difficulties and problems relating to conventional translations could have occurred, especially when one keeps in mind that God is so omnipotent, omnipresent and omniscient that He had to limit Himself in order to express Himself through man's language so that man might have a chance to begin to understand His extensiveness.

The origin of time from the dateless past

Although it is clear from scripture that God existed from all eternity (*Ps.90:2; 93:2; Pr.8:22-31; Mic.5:2; Jn.1:1-3; Heb.9:14; Rev.1:4-8*) it is certainly not clear what God did during the dateless past.

Our only knowledge is that He created the spiritual, moral and material universe during this time and since God is multi-dimensional while we are only three - dimensional, it is quite probable that we simply would not be able to fathom any additional information from the dateless past that would give us more clarity regarding the history before time, as we know it, commenced.

The dateless past (*Pr.8:22-23; Jn.1:1; Acts 15:18; Eph.3:9; Col.1:18; Heb.1:10, 1Jn.1:1; Rev.1:6 & Rev.3:14*) is that period which is referred to in Genesis. 1:1 *"In the beginning God created the heaven and the earth."*

Verse 1 is the introduction to the whole Bible and all history, for it marks the boundary between "time" and "eternity". It is not a summarized statement of what is to follow, for it mentions heaven first, while the following versus mention the earth first. *Job 38: 4-7* makes it clear that the heavens were created first otherwise the stars could not have rejoiced when the earth was created.

This proves that Genesis chapter 1, verse 1 refers to prior acts of God and the verses which follow refer to the earth under a flood and judgement, and then restored to a second habitable state, as before the curse of verse 2.

As such, verse 1 refers to the time of the pre-Adamite world before sin and rebellion caused Lucifer's flood that is referred to in verse 2. Lucifer's flood was more devastating and lasted longer than the flood that occurred during Noah's time which destroyed even the vegetation as is clear from *Gen.2:5-6*.

This passage also refers to the time before man and plants were created. The Hebrew word, bara, is defined as to bring into being, directly translated into English as the word "create". This word is used 7 times in *Gen.1-2*, whereas in all other places the words "made" and "make" are used.

This proves that God's 6 days' to have been mainly reconstructive and restorative. In *Gen.1:1* the universe is brought into existence, in *Gen.1:21* sea creatures are created and in *Gen.1:27* man is created. Thus the Hebrew word, *bara,* or the English word "create" is reserved for the introduction of these three great spheres of existence, being the world of matter, natural life as in all living creatures and spiritual life represented by man.

In *Gen.1:16* the word "made" is used instead of the word "create" because these bodies had been created before the earth was and were forbidden to give light on earth during the chaos caused by Lucifer's rebellion until judgement had been completed *(Isa.14:12-14; Jer.4:23-26; Ezek.28:11 and 2 Pet.3:5-8).*

The original creations of God include the heavens, the earth and all things therein as first brought into being. They were made perfect the first time. *Gen.1:1* refers to the dateless past or the beginning of the creative ages *(Acts 17:24-26; Col.1:15-18; Heb.1:1-12; Rev.4:11).*

The 6 days of re-creation in *Gen.1:3* up to *2:25* are a part of and the end of the creative ages.

"And God said, Let there be light in the firmament of the heaven to divide the day from the night; and let them be for signs, and for seasons, and for days and years:"

Genesis 1:14

Time must have existed during Lucifer's reign, in the dateless past, and before the earth was made void due to his sin and rebellion. Concerning our own circumstances and what is pertinent regarding God's plan, however, in relation to time, we should refrain from wasting too much energy trying to determine when the exact beginning evidently occurred. With the above in mind we find it altogether impossible to determine when time commenced. God is after all, eternal. For the purposes of God's pre-determined plan for us, pertaining to His times and seasons through the ages we should narrow our focus from that point in time when man was created.

We can be fairly certain that times and seasons pertaining to mankind, through the ages of God, were brought into existence with the creation of Adam and more particularly after the fall of man in the Garden of Eden.

Although times and seasons with regards to earth are physically regulated by the heavenly bodies created by God, when God refers to the times and seasons concerning man, it is spiritual by nature and refers to the various times, events and tests that God has planned for our lives. Before we examine God's times and seasons pertaining to our personal lives, let us first take a look at the various ages in time that can be determined through Scripture, in order to enable us to better understand what is in store for mankind as a whole.

The various ages through time

A universal approach towards times and seasons:

The word "*age*" as a noun, is defined as the length of time that a person has lived, or a thing has existed, or a distinct period of history.
The Hebrew word *eth* and the Greek word *aion* mean any period of time whether long or short; time or season. In this sense there are numberless ages *(Job 38:23; Eccl.3:1-17; Isa.49:8; Dan.8:17; Eph.2:7)* which are categorized as:

- the past ages *(Job 8:8; Isa.45:21; Ezek.26:20; Lk.1:70; Acts 3:21; Col.1:26),*
- the present age *(Mt.13:22; Mk.4:19; Lk.16:8; Rom.12:2; Gal.1:4),*
- the future ages *(Mt.12:31-32; Mk.10:30; Lk.20:35; Eph.1:21; 1 Tim.1:17),* and
- the creative ages *(Gen.1:1 – 2:25; Rom.1:20; Eph.3:9; Col.1:15-18).*

According to Dake's Annotated Reference Bible there are five main ages throughout time that we recognize throughout Scripture:

- The ante – chaotic age
- The ante – diluvian age
- The present or post diluvian age
- The age to come
- The age of the ages

By means of a summary of the information available from pages 58 – 62 in Dake's Annotated Reference Bible, let us take a more detailed look at the various ages:

- The ante – chaotic age

This was the age from the original creation in *Gen.1:1* until chaos reigned as in Gen.1:2. It was the time when Lucifer ruled the earth in perfection, before he fell and made the earth chaotic and flooded *(Isa.14:12-14; Jer.4:23-26; Ezek.28:11-17; Lk.10:18; 2 Pet.3:5-8).*
This age consisted of the whole period from the dateless past, the original creations, Lucifer's reign in perfection *(Ezek.28:15)*, his period of rebellion and the pre – Adamites, the actual war between heaven and earth which in turn culminated in the defeat of Lucifer and his armies as they invaded heaven *(Isa.14:12-14)* and the chaotic period on earth after the defeat of Lucifer's kingdom *(Jer.4:23-26).*

These periods were of unknown length and could also be called the eternal past. During this period angels, and not men, were given rulership under God to administer His will and rule the earth *(Col.1:15-18; 1 Pet.3:22; Rev.12:7-10; Rev.20:10).*

God's purpose was to test the angels to see whether they would remain true to Him as trusted servants before using them eternally. For the same reason God tested man.

Lucifer was the first to be exalted in pride; and he and his angelic followers were the first to attempt to overthrow God's government. If they had remained true to God there would have been no flood and chaos as in *Gen.1:2* and therefore no need of the 6 days of *Gen.1:3-2:25* to restore the earth to a second habitable state, and no need for the creation of new land animals, fish, fowls and man to rule the planet earth. Lucifer and the pre – Adamites would have continued to live on the earth and carry out the plan of dominion over the earth designed for man.

The entire Bible message centres around the complete redemption of man, which includes ridding the earth of all rebellion, so that in the new heavens and new earth, the original state of the universal Kingdom of God will be fully restored, and God will be all in all eternally *(Eph.1:10; Rev. 21-22)*.

When Adam rebelled the earth entered its second sinful career. In God's plan we are now probably nearing the end of Adam's rebellion as God is soon to send Jesus Christ together with the armies of heaven to defeat the armies of Antichrist and seize the governments of this world.

This will be done with the express purpose of setting up a righteous government on earth forever and the first 1000 years (Millennium) of the eternal kingdom will be for the purpose of putting down all rebellion once and for all. God's sovereignty will be restored entirely.

- The ante – diluvian age

The age from the beginning of the six days of restoration of the heavens and earth *(Gen.1:2)* to a second habitable state ending with the flood during Noah's time *(Gen.6:8 – 8:14).*

This was the age where man was tested and put on probation while in innocence. God wanted to see whether man would remain innocent and true to his trust under the most favourable and perfect conditions possible.

God wanted to test man before he had offspring, so that if he sinned the entire race could be dealt with alike through the same means of grace which offers redemption to all who desire it wholeheartedly. Man was tested to see whether he would obey his own conscience regarding right and wrong and the purpose of God was to guide him in the proper exercise of his conscience to do right and refuse the wrong.

Fallen man would be taught that only by obedience to God and His will, would he be restored to his original dominion and be freed from the curse. God wanted man to see that he was powerless to cope in his fallen state, to be brought to helplessness in himself so that he would turn to God for help, grace and power against sin, to overcome the curse he brought upon himself.

- Present or post – diluvian age

This is the age from the flood of Noah *(Gen.6:8 – 8:14-15)* to the Millennium *(Rev.19:10-11; Rev.20:7)* and can be further divided into four dispensational periods:

The first was the period during which human laws and governments were instituted to regulate man after a long age of freedom of conscience.

Man was given certain laws to govern the race by and held responsible for self – government, lasting from the flood during Noah's time to the call of Abraham.

God wanted to test man under a new standard of conduct by forcing him to obey the right and reject the wrong through the obedience of the laws of human government and to rule faithfully. Various governments were established by God and man was responsible to rule for the greater good of all.

Second was the period in which the promises and covenants were made with Abraham and his seed and lasted from the call of Abraham when he was approximately 75 years old until the exodus from Egypt *(Ex.12:40; Gal.3:14-17).*

God began to deal with a specific branch of the race in fulfilment of His plan, the test was to have faith in God, obey Him, remain segregated from other nations and evangelize the world.

God's purpose was to choose one man through whom the Messiah would come. To use him and his seed as His representatives in the earth. The call of God, the covenants and promises, and the personal dealings of God, were His means in fulfilling His plan with Israel.

The third period was when the law was given unto Moses which became part of the rule of faith and practice during the period between Moses and Christ. This lasted from the exodus from Egypt to the preaching of the Kingdom of Heaven by John the Baptist *(Mt.11:12-13; Lk.16:16).*

The test was to see if they would obey the law of Moses in every detail, as the law was a foreshadow of the good things to come and was added because of transgressions until the Seed should come.

By the giving of the law and the setting of Israel in the Promised Land and to use them as an outstanding nation, God wanted to display the benefits of serving the One and only true God.

The fourth period is the age during which the fullness of grace was brought about by Jesus Christ, commencing with the preaching of John the Baptist *(Mt.11:11)* and will last until the second coming of Christ.

The test is whether man will be able to stay obedient to the faith in the gospel and all its teachings *(Mk.16:16; Jn.3:16; Rom.1:5; Heb.11:6).* The purpose of God was to save all who would believe, to call out a people for His namesake and to build the Church *(Acts 15:13-18; 1 Cor.1:18-24; Eph.2:14-22; 2 Pet.3:9; Rev.22:17).*

As a race who form part of God's master plan we are now at a stage in history more specifically referred to as the "Time of the Gentiles" as also referred to in *Lk.21:24.* The times of the Gentiles is the time when the gentiles are utilized as a rod of chastening upon Israel to further God's purpose concerning them.

It began with Israel's first oppression by the Gentiles in Egypt and will continue up until the return of the Messiah in glory when He will deliver Israel from the Gentiles and exalt them as the head of all nations in the Millennium and forever *(Rom.11:25; Rev.19:11-20).*

According to the website: "Kingdom Watcher" (www.kingwatch.co.nz) the majority of the Jews are absent from the Kingdom during this period because they have rejected the Messiah as a nation and are under judgement.

This is one of the reasons why the Kingdom does not reach fulfilment as the Kingdom of God cannot be complete while one of the nations is excluded from it.

Even though Satan was cast out of heaven *(Rev.12:13)* he does have a legal right on earth through the Jews who are under judgement and because the Jews are scattered among the nations he has been able to work his evil in all the nations.
The times of the Gentiles will come to an end when the judgement of the Jews is complete and then we will see a rapid advance of the Kingdom of God.

"Yea, the stork in the heaven knoweth her appointed times; and the turtle and the crane and the swallow observe the time of their coming, but my people know not the judgement of the Lord."

Jeremiah 8:7

The other stage which has not yet come to pass, is the "Times of the Kingdom".

- The age to come

Referred to in *Mt.12:32* as well as *Eph.1:21*, this is the age where Divine Government will take over all human governments. The first 1000 years of God's rule on earth is also called the Millennium *(Rev.20:1-10)*.

This period will last from the second advent of Christ, when the battle of Armageddon and the judgement of nations will take place, until the renovation of the heavens and the earth and the beginning of the new heavens and earth after 1000 years *(Rev.20:1-15; 21:1; 2 Pet.3:10-13).*

For the first time since Adam submitted to Lucifer, his fallen angels and demons, man will be free from them and have perfect earthly conditions in every respect as before the Fall, since Satan will be bound at the start of this age *(Mt.24:29-31; Mt.25:31-46; Rev.19:11-20).*

During this age, however, man will still be subjected to death when he commits any sin carrying the death penalty. Even though human instincts, tendencies and lusts will still be a part of human nature, these will be easier to overcome since there will be no satanic power or influence.

Christ and the resurrected saints will be reigning over the coming generations from the beginning of the Millennium into eternity. The test during this period would be for the resurrected saints to obey Christ, comply with civil and religious laws of the kingdom and conform to the will of God *(Isa.2:2-4; Zech.14:11-21; Rev.5:10; 11:15; 20:1-10).*

The purpose of God would be to bring about the following:

- finally put down all remaining rebellion,
- to fulfil the everlasting covenants from the past,
- vindicate and avenge Christ and the saints,
- exalt the resurrected saints of all ages to a kingly and priestly position,
- judge the nations in righteousness,
- restore the earth to its rightful owners,
- and restore Israel as the head of all nations.

All enemies need to be put under the feet of Christ to restore the perfect conditions that existed before the fall Lucifer and man.
At the end of the Millennium, Satan will be loosed from the bottomless pit and multitudes will openly rebel, by trying to overthrow God's government yet again, albeit for the last time *(Rev.20:7-10).*

At this point in time God will bring an end to all rebellion in His Universal Kingdom by bringing judgement upon all human rebels and while righteous men and angels will serve God, assisting Him in administering the affairs of the universe forever *(Dan.2:44-45; Dan.7:13-14; Gen.8:22; Gen.9:12).*

"For the vision is yet for an appointed time, but at the end it shall speak, and not lie: though it tarry, wait for it; because it will surely come, it will not tarry."

Habakkuk 2:3

- The age of the ages

So – called because resurrected saints and faithful angels will be helping God to administer the affairs of the universe from the earth which will be the eternal headquarters of His government in a timeless age which we know as the New Heaven and the New Earth or Eternal Future and will be without end.

There will be no further need for moral or probationary tests to see whether man or angels will prove true and worthy of eternal trust as all would have been purged from all possibility of falling. All will be obedient to God's laws and will and will be absolutely and eternally trusted by God *(Heb.1:13; Heb.2:9-18; Zech.14:1-5; Mt.13:38-51; Rev.19:11-21).*

The purpose of God will be, to be all in all again, as before the rebellion began with Lucifer and Adam, and to carry out His eternal plan of having creatures who are willingly subject to Him and consecrated to the same end that He is, which is the highest good of being for all in all the universe *(Rev.22:3-5).*

"And He said unto them, it is not for you to know the times or the seasons, which the Father hath put in His own power."

Acts 1:7

A personal approach towards times and seasons:
All the above - mentioned details pertains to the universal times and seasons which will affect the human race as a whole during a course of events in which God's masterplan for the universe will be brought to fruition.
With this in mind it is extremely important to remember that we serve a God Who is very detailed meaning that He also has the finest plans and purposes laid out for each and every individual. All these individual plans form part of the collective effort to establish His Kingdom.

It is we as individuals, who will also experience the best laid plans through our own times and seasons, as ordained by God Himself. For these individual plans of God to materialize we will need to achieve certain milestones with regards to our faith, obedience, gratefulness, love, humility, joy and overall attitude in our personal relationship with the Holy Trinity.

For each and every individual God has pre – determined a specific calling to advance His Kingdom which will be realized through the times and seasons in one's life.

"Blessed is the man that endureth temptation: for when he is tried, he shall receive the crown of life, which the Lord hath promised to them that love Him."

James 1:12

You will require proper training to be successful in the calling that the Creator of the universe has bestowed upon you in order to be victorious against the relentless onslaughts of the enemy. This is accompanied by the different tests, trials and tribulations everyone experiences throughout their lives.

Our personal relationship towards God and the world will determine whether we honestly learn and grow stronger in Christ during each particular season and whether we remain standing after the fact.
God's outlook and His idea of breakthrough or victory are so monumentally different from ours, that we would certainly fail to meet His standards given our inclination to attempt everything through our own power.

"And let us not be weary in well doing: for in due season we shall reap, if we faint not."

Galatians 6:9

Moreover, being a believer in Christ is not static, so one needs to grow constantly. To stand in a personal relationship with God is a dynamic process that should be evolving all the time.

The closer we move to God, the more we grow, and the more we grow, the easier we heed to our various callings.

In God's plan He makes provision for us to grow in Him during the times and seasons in our lives. God wants us to learn during these times so that we might stand firm against the enemy in victory.

True children of God will never surrender and will always advance, no matter how dire the consequences or unbearable the odds. Far too many Christians are under the impression that once they are converted and possibly, baptized, that life simply goes on regardless.

As long as they go to church on a Sunday and proclaim to believe in Christ, once in a while, they think that they are saved. This is very far from the truth and it is in fact much harder to fully surrender to God's will, and to unshakably walk in the ways of the Lord than many contemporary proclaim.

The truth is that the closer we move towards the heart of God, the greater and more frequent the attacks from the enemy occur, because, we are now also a bigger threat to his kingdom of eternal suffering.

"My times are in thy hand: deliver me from the hand of mine enemies, and from them that persecute me."

Psalm 31:15

The good news is that the more intimate we are with Christ, the easier it becomes to withstand these onslaughts.

It is reasonable to assume that the enemy will not waste his time to cause the unrighteous and unholy to fall as they are already lost and will only really start to take notice, once they are converted.

That is why the enemy focusses all his energy on the righteous, in an attempt to cause them to fall and thus foil God's plans for dominion of the earth. Too many Christians utter the words: "I am just a Christian, I am not perfect" too often as an excuse for their own deliberate shortcomings or backslidings.

God will never be content with second best and that is why He wants to equip us to be the best that we can possibly be through His planned times and seasons for us. The idea then, is to endure and persevere through times of trial and tribulation and to gain Godly wisdom and righteousness in the appointed seasons through our constant and obedient seeking of His ultimate will and purpose for our lives by which we inadvertently become part of His miraculous solution.

"There hath no temptation taken you but such as is common to man: but God is faithful, who will not suffer you to be tempted above that ye are able; but will with the temptation also make a way to escape, that ye may be able to bear it."

1 Corinthians 10:13

Nothing ever happens out of coincidence, as everything happens for a reason. Either because Father God has ordained specific events, or because the legal right obtained by the enemy through one's unrepented sin, He had to allow certain events.

The closer we move to God the more clearly we will see His hand move in our lives and the further away we move from God the more we will be controlled by, and become reliant on the world.

It is simple; if we move, God moves. Bearing in mind that we obviously have to move in the rightly ordained direction in the first place. However, just it requires honest and dedicated prayers first, before angels react on our behalf, so God will only move once we are consecrated to Him and seek His presence out of our own free will.

Through our times and seasons we are equipped to stand strong and fight the good fight, by which we develop into mature sons and daughters of the Almighty One. Everything we do and every action in which we partake, is done by being seated in Him.

"Even when we were dead in sins, hath quickened us together with Christ, (by grace ye are saved;) And hath raised us up together, and made us sit together in heavenly places in Christ Jesus:
That in the ages to come he might shew the exceeding riches of His grace in His kindness toward us through Christ Jesus."

Ephesians 2:5-7

According to a blog by Jennifer LeClaire, the news editor at Charisma Magazine, we often resist transition into a new season just because we are ignorant, immature or simply fear change. We need to remember that failing to move in God's timing can bring unwanted consequences. It is imperative that you prophetically discern both the times and seasons you are in, by moving with the Holy Spirit.

Jennifer further states that it is not always easy to transition from one season to another even in the best of circumstances. The key to transitioning well is to first discern the change in season.
Staying prayerful and exploring prophetic words that were spoken over your life will help you distinguish between the work of the Holy Spirit and the work of the enemy in your life.

Once you have discerned that the Lord is ushering you into a new season you need to quickly get into agreement with Him. Surrender your will to the Lord's will and be sensitive to the leading of the Holy Spirit. When you do, you will find peace and joy even in the midst of the most difficult transitions.

When you resist the will of the Lord you find yourself without the grace you need to rise to the occasion He is calling you to. He gives grace to the humble and supplies plentiful mercy to the grateful and devoted. It does not matter what season you are in now or what season the Lord has planned for you next, you should remain encouraged. Seasons may change and winds may blow, but God is the God of all seasons.

"For I know the thoughts that I think toward you, saith the Lord, thoughts of peace, and not of evil, to give you an expected end."

Jeremiah 29:11

Our Heavenly Father will never ever force you to be devoted to Him and will never completely reveal His will and purpose for your life if both our feet are not firmly planted within His Kingdom.

Many people want to serve God with one foot planted in the world and one in the Kingdom, or even worse, both feet continuously stumbling around in the world. As such, they have been severely misled by the enemy, mostly out of fear, and fail to comprehend that an all-powerful God has the perfect plan for each of them.

You should fear God only, but unfortunately many are being misled to fear the world instead, while the real power behind being misled is that one doesn't know that one is being misled.

You cannot be fully committed to God if you do not fully trust in Him, as you certainly cannot serve Him on our own terms and conditions. The core idea behind weathering the storms of life within your own personal times and seasons is not merely to enable you to remain standing and advancing against the enemy, but also to gain the heart of wisdom to discern His will and purpose for you.

God requires total personal devotion from the perspective of your own free will and if you really believe with all your hearts that the Father knows exactly what you need, you will always put Him first. Putting God first also means trusting Him with your whole heart, mind and soul and that you believe unwaveringly that no matter what the world might say, your Creator always knows best.

God will test you, frequently, to discern your trust in Him and to build your character through obedience, humility and faith. He will never forsake His loved ones, rather it is we, who forsake Him.

When you are going through a time of discomfort, inconvenience or struggles, you should take joy in knowing that your Father has also ordained the breakthrough, provided you remain focused on Him. In these victories you come closer to reaching your callings that were bestowed upon you from before the foundations of the earth were set.
It is extremely comforting and awe - inspiring to know that in spite of your utter significance, it is in God's will and purpose that you as an individual have a part in implementing His master plan; that all mankind might be deemed worthy to share in His eternal peace and glory.

With eternity being engraved upon your heart, you irrevocably believe that God will do the righteous thing at the right time. And should impossible elements be present, you are assured that God is always near. This does not mean that you will always understand God's infinite wisdom or even comprehend His plan, but it does mean that His ever - presence will fill us with an enduring inner - peace that will overcome all odds.

"See then that ye walk circumspectly, not as fools, but as wise,
Redeeming the time because the days are evil.
Wherefore be ye not unwise, but understanding what the will of the Lord is."

Ephesians 5:15-17

According to a teaching by Andy Stanley entitled "Time of your life", you should always be asking the question what are you doing with your time as time is running out since your days are numbered.

He says that you should always spend your time with the end in mind, seeing your life within God's context. The greatest opportunity you have during the swiftness of your life is to live within God's context and to become fully reliant on His will and purpose for yourself.

When everything is about you and you deteriorate into self-absorption, you will never learn how to live your life as if your days are numbered and you will continuously try to fill a material void in which you are the centre of your own universe.

The key, according to Andy, is to prioritize. Priority determines the capacity of your time and truly putting God first is an excellent start to where exactly your priorities lie.

Most importantly, if you continue to neglect your walk with God, especially after conversion, the negative impact on your life will be cumulative. Just as the priority to spend personal time with the Lord in earnestness will bring about compounding blessings and rewards, the opposite is also true.

If you want to know to what extent God is manifesting through your lifes it would be to what extent, you exercise self-control and experience the Godly peace and joy that goes beyond all human understanding. Although we serve a loving, merciful and faithful God, He is also to the point and serious, demanding discipline and obedience. Saving souls from eternal damnation is a serious matter.

"Lord, thou hast been our dwelling place in all generations.
Before the mountains were brought forth, or ever thou hadst formed the earth and the world, even from everlasting to everlasting, thou art God.
Thou turnest man to destruction; and sayest, Return, ye children of men.
For a thousand years in thy sight are but as yesterday when it is past, and as a watch in the night. Thou carriest them away as with a flood; they are as a sleep: in the morning they are like grass which growth up.
In the morning it flourisheth, and groweth up; in the evening it is cut down, and withereth.
For we are consumed by thine anger, and by thy wrath are we troubled.
Thou hast set our iniquities before thee, our secret sins in the light of thy countenance.
For all our days are passed away in thy wrath: we spend our years as a tale that is told.
These days of our years are threescore years and ten; and if by reason of strength they be fourscore years, yet is their strength labour and sorrow; for it is soon cut off, and we fly away.
Who knoweth the power of thine anger? even according to thy fear, so is thy wrath.
So teach us to number our days, that we may apply our hearts unto wisdom.
Return, O Lord, how long? and let it repent thee concerning thy servants.
O satisfy us early with thy mercy; that we may rejoice and be glad all our days.

Make us glad according to the days wherein thou hast afflicted us, and the years wherein we have seen evil.
Let thy work appear unto thy servants, and thy glory unto their children.
And let the beauty of the Lord our God be upon us: and establish thou the work of our hands upon us; yea, the work of our hands establish thou it."

Psalm 90

God has promised that He will never allow you to be tempted and tested above our own abilities. So assured, knowing that if you fully surrender to His trust, your victory is guaranteed.

With this promise in mind, you know that as a true child of God, you will refrain from any earthly excuses, and that in the eyes of the Lord failure is not an option, because if your God is for you then who can be against you.

The Lord knows exactly what you as a child of the Light are able to endure at any particular time during your period of growth in Him. That is why particular times and seasons are not always revealed in advance, lest you succumb beforehand to your own weaknesses.

At times, times and seasons are revealed to us suddenly, so that you possess the element of surprise towards the enemy. Your adversary is an extremely mighty and sly one, so without the undivided and constant intervention of Abba Father you do not have any hope whatsoever in overcoming him.

Find solace and comfort in knowing that times and seasons may come and go but our God is everlasting and will remain the same eternally. Regardless of what those in bondage to the world might say, His undying love for you will endure forever.

General information

- Anyone, within their jurisdictional right, can go to this court.
- The times and seasons of individuals, families, businesses, tribes, communities, countries, nations and the entire world are mediated through this court.
- All four seasons; winter, summer, autumn and spring are present in this court as well as all four winds; north, south, east and west.
- Court proceedings are conducted outdoors in a very colourful environment with everyone present wearing festive garments.
- The various feasts ordained by God play a part in The Court of Times and Seasons, and are always present.
- In addition, there are 24 pillars of pure gold, the purpose of which will be discussed in more detail later.

An experience

The following is an account of a personal experience in the Court of Times and Seasons by Brigette:

"The first time I had a glimpse of this court, I was in The Court of Mercy and Grace, with a king (businessman). I instinctively knew that God was going to allow us both, to go into The Court of Times and Seasons very soon.

Just as expected, a few days later, we were invited by God to enter this court with the king (businessman), his wife and two other members of our ministry. As we entered I was acutely aware of the way we were dressed.

We were dressed in the most colourful royal garments and I was a bit surprised that the king's wife's garment was almost identical to my own, until I remembered that we both carry the anointing and authority of Esther.

The thrones of Jesus and God was before us as we walked down a beautiful path covered with autumn leaves. It seemed as if we were in the middle of the most magnificent garden. I just stood amazed at the indescribable beauty.

We were surrounded by the most extraordinary trees, bearing fruits, blossoms, green and autumn leaves, simultaneously.
I also saw streams with the most enticing clear water and experienced a deep desire to drink from them.
In the distance I saw mountains with their tops covered in snow.
I was momentarily overwhelmed that were standing in the midst of all four seasons simultaneously.

A gentle breeze was blowing, and that is when I became aware that all four winds were present in this court; although their importance would only be revealed to me at a later stage.

There were 24 gold pillars along the sides of the pathway. In addition, we were surrounded by a great cloud of witnesses, all dressed in the most festive and beautiful apparel. The Holy Spirit later revealed to me that they were dressed according to God's feasts as this played a significant and prominent role in God's times and seasons.

Angels were constantly moving in and out of this court as they came back with reports and received mandates and commissions from God. Standing in front of the throne of God, the righteous Judge, with Jesus seated on a throne to His right, God immediately presented the king and his wife with a choice pertaining to the season they were about to enter.

They were informed that they were about to enter a season of oppression and tribulation but that they would mature in Him through this. They were given a choice whether they wanted to go through this season in the normal time but with a lighter burden or whether they were willing to accept a shorter season with the burdens being more intense.

God also promised to give them the necessary strength to endure and to be by their side indefinitely.

I was a bit surprised at this course of events, as I was used to pleading a case first before hearing God speak, but realised that they must have reached a certain level of maturity for God to have offered them such a choice.

This particular couple chose the shorter period, illustrating their absolute trust and confidence in God.

At that point in time I became very aware of God's hands as He created a whirlwind using the eastern and western winds, mixed with autumn and winter seasons and blew this whirlwind through the king's spirit. The breath of God immediately fortified his spirit and I instinctively understood that God was strengthening him for what lay ahead."

Interpreting the various seasons

The following is a summary of what the Holy Spirit has already revealed to us regarding the Lord's seasons. However, there is most certainly more to come, and it is very possible that God will provide further revelations to the rest of His Body in order to keep His children from becoming independent.

The most prominent elements within this court are the various seasons and winds. It is crucial to have a basic prophetic understanding of these elements as these, to a great extent, reveal what God is saying or doing.

- Winter

This is usually a time of difficulty and of great tribulation, where God may be separating or isolating you for reasons that will develop in you an absolute trust in God alone. This is also a season of rest and restoration, when you prepare for the next season.

"And I will restore to you the years that the locust hath eaten, the cankerworm, and the caterpillar, and the palmerworm, my great army which I sent among you.
And ye shall eat in plenty, and be satisfied, and praise the name of the Lord your God, that hath dealt wondrously with you: and my people shall never be ashamed."

Joel: 2:25-26

It is a time for harvest, when things might look dead and a time to burn the tares.

"Let both grow together until the harvest: and in the time of harvest I will say to the reapers, Gather ye together first the tares, and bind them in bundles to burn them: but

gather the wheat into my barn."

Matthew 13:30

- Spring

This is a time of new beginnings, a season of blossom and a time of acceleration. During this time, doors will open and acknowledgement will be received. It is also a time of innovation and a time to plant and sow.

- Summer

This is the season for growth, opportunity, new platforms and opened doors. It might also be a season of rain or no rain, depending on the scroll that was written on your life by God.

When it rains there will be an outpouring of the Holy Spirit and of God's blessings. There will be provision and growth for seeds that were sown and one will receive abundant grace and fruitfulness. The Word of God that will be poured out, will initiate growth and could lead to revival.

When there is no rain it will be a time of testing and judgement and will be a season of being in the wilderness or desert.

- Autumn

This is the season of spiritual maturity and the time when the gifts of the Holy Spirit are developed.

It can also be a time where something (a person or business) will come to an end, and can symbolize the ending of one season and the beginning of another. Associate this time with a preparation for rest, as it is also a season of completion. During this season you will reach a deeper perspective of God and should renew your commitments with Him.

"The harvest is past, the summer is ended, and we are not saved."

Jeremiah 8:20

Interpreting the various winds

Wind is the movement and breath of the Holy Spirit, the sign of Godly assurance. It also reveals that which is hidden.

"The wind hath bound her up in her wings, and they shall be ashamed because of their sacrifices."

Hosea 4:19

- Northerly Wind

This wind represents the glory and majesty of God and will powerfully awaken one to the Holy Spirit.

"And now men see not the bright light which is in the clouds: but the wind passeth, and cleanseth them.
Fair weather cometh out of the north: with God is terrible majesty."

Job 37:21-22

- Easterly Wind

"He caused an east wind to blow in the heaven: and by his power he brought in the south wind."

Psalm 78:26

This wind brings forth a time of isolation, of new beginnings, wisdom and a time when the Holy Spirit will destroy structures not ordained by God.

"And Moses stretched forth his rod over the land of Egypt, and the Lord brought an east wind upon the land all that day, and all that night; and when it was morning, the east wind brought the locusts."

Exodus 10:13

This is also a wind that will bring forth judgement. Springs and fountains will become dry, and treasures will be spoiled.

"Though he be fruitful among his brethren, an east wind shall come, the wind of the Lord shall come up from the wilderness, and his spring shall become dry, and his fountain shall be dried up: he shall spoil the treasure of all pleasant vessels."

Hosea 13:15

The easterly wind can be a warning of pending loss and may cause storms, tornadoes and hurricanes.

"The east wind carrieth him away, and he departeth: and as a storm hurleth him out of his place."

Job 27:21

- Southern Wind

"How thy garments are warm, when he quieteth the earth by the south wind?"

Job 37:17

This wind will make you experience the comfort and warmth of God but can also be a warning of possible confrontation. The southern wind is also symbolic of the enemy that brings opposition.

- Westerly Wind

"And the Lord turned a mighty strong west wind, which took away the locusts, and cast them into the Red sea; there remained not one locust in all the coasts of Egypt."

Exodus 10:19

This wind brings forth the promise of blessings, redemption and transformation, enabling you to resist the destroyer.

- Whirlwinds

"Then the Lord answered Job out of the whirlwind, and said,"

Job 38:1

"Then answered the Lord unto Job out of the whirlwind, and said,"

Job 40:6

We will find the voice of God within the whirlwind. It is created to bring about spiritual change in a person, situation, community, country or nation.

Interpreting time gates

"That in blessing I will bless thee, and in multiplying I will multiply thy seed as the stars of the heaven, and as the sand which is upon the sea shore; and thy seed shall possess the gate of his enemies."

Genesis 22:17

Within every season there are various times and phases. And within every cycle there are different seasons. Several cycles form an era.

To move from one phase to another, one season to another, or from one era to another, you will need to pass through time gates. Even in every 24- hour day, there are different phases and watches. More often than not, the Holy Spirit will awaken you at a specific hour, to watch and pray within a specific watch.

"And if he shall come in the second watch, or come in the third watch, and find them so, blessed are those servants."

Luke 12:38

These time gates are often controlled by the enemy. Where he is in possession of a time gate that leads to the next phase, season, cycle or era, he will certainly influence it to the children of the Light's detriment. Although the children of God received all authority to possess these gates, due to a lack of knowledge you may not be in control of them. However, there are appointed individuals or ministries who stand in a specific position of authority as gatekeepers for a family, business, ministry, community, city or country. This topic is discussed in more detail in the book *"International Guarding Operations and Training Manual Volume 1"* by Haima Christou Ministries.

"And the porters, Akkub, Talmon and their brethren that kept the gates, were an hundred seventy two."
1 Chronicles 9:17

It is of vital importance that the Body of Christ awakens to be ever watchful against an enemy who is relentlessly pursuing to change the times and seasons.

"And he shall speak great words against the most High, and think to change times and laws: and they shall be given into his hand until a time and times and the dividing of time."

Daniel 7:25

Interpreting the golden pillars

There are twenty - four golden pillars located in the court of Times and Seasons, with each pillar representing an hour of the day.

These pillars symbolise a very significant anointing and authority, and therefore it is imperative for you to understand the hour you move in and specifically the type of authority and anointing for that hour.

The message within each hour may contain warnings and so you need to rely on the Holy Spirit to reveal to you the whole message in its entirety. Keep in mind that there is a god over every hour in the "New Age" world which serves as a counterfeit to what God had already ordained pertaining to the hours of each day. Satan is the master counterfeiter and the line between what is right and what is wrong becomes impossibly thin without the guidance and support of the Holy Spirit.

Numerous occult rituals are continuously practiced in which curses are spoken over each hour, day, month, year and decade in an effort by the enemy to gain control over the times.

Although we should never be totally oblivious to what the enemy is up to, we should rather always focus our attention on what God is doing.
Interpreting the twenty – four hours

The following is an explanation of the various hours in each day, contrasted with the possible counterfeit from the enemy that was revealed to us by the Spirit. The first hour starts at 24h00:

- 1st Hour:

A time of commencement, unity and complete agreement with the Holy Spirit and others. This hour also represents the one true God.
We need to be alert for the enemy not to mislead us with independence and spiritual blindness during this hour. Satan might also attempt to establish himself as "god".

- 2nd Hour:

An hour of agreement between God and man as well as the children of the Light among one another. It reflects a time of brotherhood, testimony and witness.

Christ always sent His disciples in pairs to perform their missions; to help and protect one another and to bear one another's burdens. Where two are in agreement there is also a fulfilment of one of Christ's laws.

"Again I say unto you, That if two of you shall agree on earth as touching any thing that they shall ask, it shall be done for them of my Father which is in heaven."

Matthew 18:19

The enemy will persist in trying to bring division during this hour.

- 3rd Hour:

This hour represents a time of perfect and divine completion and the fullness of the Godhead: Father, Son and Holy Spirit. While it carries an anointing of harmony, the enemy's counterfeit would be to bring strife which creates cycles that may lead to failure and annulment.

- 4th Hour:

An hour in which there is an anointing and authority to create as well as divine protection. This is also the hour of revival through which God's Kingdom should come to earth.

Be cautious not to conform to the world, as the enemy will press forward to establish world powers and rule within this hour.

- 5th Hour:

The hour in which there is the anointing of multiplication, provision and miraculous power. This is also the hour in which we will find more intimacy with God and hence probably the best time to seek God's presence.

"My voice shalt thou hear in the morning, O Lord; in the morning will I direct my prayer unto thee, and will look up."

Psalm 5:3

This intimacy is observed in the measurements of the Tabernacle which were mostly multiples of five. During this hour we should align with the God of grace and be strengthened as the enemy will release the religious spirit to instil punishment and legalism. The enemy will also attempt to bring a curse of unfruitfulness.

- 6th Hour:

Man was created on the 6th day and therefore this hour is associated with a time in which things are fulfilled in the physical dimension. It is also a time of completing Godly ordained tasks. From the enemies' perspective six refers to the anti-Christ, slavery, imperfect government and sin.

- 7th Hour:

This is an hour of perfection, completion and rest; an hour in which righteousness will prevail. This hour carries a sevenfold blessing through Jesus Christ, namely: power, riches, wisdom, strength, honour, glory and blessing.

"Saying with a loud voice, Worthy is the Lamb that was slain to receive power, and riches, and wisdom and strength, and honour, and glory, and blessing."

Revelation 5:12

This time also carries the anointing of humility, purification (to be purified seven times seven, like silver), and that of the servant.

During this hour the seven Spirits of God (the Spirit of the Lord, the Spirit of wisdom and understanding, the Spirit of counsel and might, the Spirit of knowledge and the fear of the Lord); and the seven redemptive gifts of the Holy Spirit are released, is present and manifest.

"Having then gifts differing according to the grace that is given to us, whether prophecy, let us prophesy according to the proportion of faith;
Or ministry, let us wait on our ministering: or he that teacheth, on teaching;
Or he that exhorteth, on exhortation: he that giveth, let him do it with simplicity; he that ruleth, with diligence; he that sheweth mercy, with cheerfulness."

Romans 12:6-8

This hour also represents the seven feasts of God and marks an hour of celebration and victory.

The enemy will attempt to defile this hour by bringing rebellion against God, and may reflect the seven abominations referred to in *Prov.26:25* and the seven forms of suffering of *Rom. 8:35.* They are tribulation, distress, persecution, famine, nakedness, peril and the sword.

The plagues and seven golden bowls of the wrath of God in *Rev. 15:1&7* are also symbolised by this hour.

- 8th Hour:

This is known as the hour of Immanuel (God with us). It carries the anointing of abundance, righteousness, peace and breakthrough.

The enemy may implement new demonic cycles through ancestral worship and in the world of darkness, Venus is represented by the number 8.

- 9th Hour:

The hour of the anointing of the nine gifts of the Holy Spirit.

"For to one is given by the Spirit the word of wisdom; to another the word of knowledge by the same Spirit;
To another faith by the same Spirit; to another gifts of healing by the same Spirit;
To another the working of miracles; to another prophecy; to another discerning of spirits; to another divers kinds of tongues; to another the interpretation of tongues:"

1 Corinthians 12:8-10

This is also a time for harvest, praise and worship. On the other hand, it may also speak of man's final hour when he will be judged.

- 10th Hour:

The hour in which we will find the anointing for perfection of the divine law and order, and a time of restoration.
Negatively, it may be an hour of trial and can present a time of judgement (for example, the 10 plagues that occurred in Egypt prior to the exodus of the Hebrews).

- 11th Hour:

The hour of faithfulness (11 faithful disciples) and fertility.
The enemy will bring conflict and disaster, as eleven is symbolic of the casting of black magic spells and curses.

- 12th Hour:

This hour represents governmental perfection and unity, also the authority to lay foundations (apostolic and prophetic authority) and the opening or possession of gates as referred to in *Rev. 12:14.*
During this time the anointing of the twelve tribes of Israel is released upon those who seek God diligently and walk in His ways.

The enemy seeks to defile this hour through the worship, and subsequent releasing of power by the New Age queen of heaven, as stated in *Rev. 12:1.*

- 13th Hour:

This is a time of testing which the enemy will manipulate this time to produce bitterness and rebellion against God through a lack of faith.

- 14th Hour:

This hour is a perfect cycle; a time of spiritual perfection and redemption.

"So all the generations from Abraham to David are fourteen generations; and from David until the carrying away into Babylon are fourteen generations; and from the carrying away into Babylon unto Christ are fourteen generations."

Matthew 1:17

- 15th Hour:

The hour of hope, inspiration and extended grace.

- 16th Hour:

The hour of accountability and an hour in which we build Godly character.

The sixteen works of the flesh as referred to in *1 Corinthians 12:19-21* can be negatively associated with this hour.

- 17th Hour:

Rightful inheritance is released within this hour as well as spiritual order.

- 18th Hour:

The hour in which healing and physical restoration takes place and God's righteous judgement against sin.

During this hour the enemy will try to bring shame, sickness, unfruitfulness and will come as a thief to pilfer and destroy.

- 19th Hour:

This is the hour to experience the call to worship God in spirit and in truth.

- 20th Hour:

This is an hour of reward but also a call to prepare for warfare and may refer to a time of trial and tribulation.

- 21st Hour:

Spiritual maturity, purification and an understanding of the Godhead is associated with this hour.

It is also the hour in which spiritual strongholds and principalities should be overthrown.

- 22nd Hour:

This time is consecrated to God and have authority to uproot evil.

- 23rd Hour:

There is perfect harmony with God and there is a call to minister for God's Kingdom. Authority is received to advance and to establish. The enemy may bring the works of Belial and Jezebel against you during this hour in an attempt to discourage you in your ministry.

- 24th Hour:

This hour presents a higher form of governance. The twenty - four Elders around the throne of God in the Supreme Court (Mount Zion) represents perfect governance with each Elder representing a specific anointing and authority.

Satan will fight relentlessly and endlessly to gain control of this hour, to establish his reign on earth.

The relevance

Everything, whether it is the timeline of an individual's life, a family bloodline, a business, country or nation, is pre – programmed by God in a specific manner, which is built into the various DNA's.
Cycles are established within your life, your businesses, your communities and nation as a whole through these timelines which the enemy continuously endeavours to corrupt through the legal right he receives from your sins and transgressions.

It is the Lord's desire for you to have and maintain the DNA of His Son, Jesus Christ; and for you to live according to His ordained times and seasons, through which you can reach the fullness of your destiny on earth. This in turn, will determine your eternal future.

A profound, yet simple message, spoken by the Holy Spirit said the following: "If eternity was an ocean, and your life on earth was one drop of water, then that one drop of water determines your ocean."
The relevance for the you as an individual, business, ministry and nation is to align your family's times and seasons with God's timing; and to remove the enemy's legal right to influence your times and seasons.

In order to break demonic cycles and re-programme the various DNA's to that of Jesus Christ, parents can stand proxy for their children's timelines and business leaders and ministries can stand in proxy for their employees or members already employed as well as employees and members still to be employed. They can also obtain God - inspired strategy for a specific time and season.

Business leaders and ministries can stand proxy for clients, partners, individuals, families and business timelines; and even for those yet to come and also to initiate Godly change. According to jurisdictional rights, in order to break demonic cycles over all spheres of influence, whether a business, ministry, church or community.

Exactly the same principles can be applied to nations, countries and even the world, albeit on a much grander scale.

Fig. 4: The Court of Times and Seasons

The International Court

"I saw in the night visions, and, behold, one like the Son of man came with the clouds of heaven, and came to the Ancient of days, and they brought him near before him. And there was given him dominion, and glory, and a kingdom, that all people, nations, and languages, should serve him: his dominion is an everlasting dominion, which shall not pass away, and his kingdom that which shall not be destroyed."

Daniel 7:13-1

General information

- From His throne, seated to the right of the Father, Jesus rules over all nations.
- This Court is housed inside a building that resembles the old Greek courts.
- In order to have jurisdiction for this Court, you need international authority in any of the spheres of influence.
- There is a continual debate taking place between those representing the Kingdom of Light and those representing the kingdom of darkness.
- As you will be exposed to principalities and rulers of darkness with international jurisdiction, only enter this Court when you possess the absolute certainty that you are being led by the Holy Spirit.
- Once you are certain of the Holy Spirit's prompting, you should boldly enter the International Court.
- Knowing that you will be protected through the Lord's mandates, appear with fearlessness.

An experience

"I was recently mandated by the Lord to appear in the International Court, while collaborating with two other children of God, one of whom possesses international authority as a gatekeeper.

The Holy Spirit informed us that the enemy was attempting to establish two major spiritual gates (portals) at strategic places in the world. The Lord needed the enemy's plans to be thwarted by sealing up these portals.

On entering, we were immediately asked by the Lord whether we were in agreement that these portals should be shut, and whether we were willing to represent this cause. Up until that point in time, we had not yet said anything ourselves.

On being prompted by the Lord's question, the following scripture immediately sprang to mind:

"Also I heard the voice of the Lord, saying, Whom shall I send, and who will go for us? Then said I, Here am I; send me."

Isaiah 6:8

We all agreed in unison, that we were willing.

Although it was clear to me that the Lord had already decided the outcome, He needed the Ecclesia within the appropriate God-given international authority to agree, and for the prophets to reveal and prophecy His verdict. After this was done, judgement was released, manifesting in both realms the spiritual and natural realms".

In another case;

"A businessman received Holy Spirit-inspired dreams in which he was warned that the enemy planned to hinder international funds from entering into his kingdom.

The enemy was using the influence he laid claim to through a legal right in the worldly systems, to cause delays and obstacles pertaining to a breakthrough with regard to those funds. These funds were part of the plan and purpose that God had intended for this business.

We enquired of the Lord how to address the situation, and were prompted by the Holy Spirit to commence proceedings within the Court of Mercy and Grace, from where we would receive authority to enter the International Court to present our case.

At that point in time we did not yet have the full authority to intercede for these worldly systems, so those who represented the Kingdom of Light (being in position on earth, together with those forming part of the Cloud of Witnesses) possessing and applying the right authority, assisted us by being in agreement concerning this matter.

Again we had the opportunity to witness how children of God work together in perfect unity for the will and purposes of God to be established on earth. We knew irrevocably that we were simply not meant to work independently from the Body of Christ".

"Behold, how good, and how pleasant it is for brethren to dwell together in unity!"

Psalm 133:1

An interpretation

The same interpretation discussed in the earlier section pertaining to the Parliamentary Court applies to this Court, albeit with an added requirement of international jurisdiction for continents and the world.

The relevance

This Court is particularly relevant to any individual, ministry, church, or business with an international authority. It is through this Court that righteous governments are to be established on earth.

Children of God who have jurisdictional right to operate within this Court, should apply their positions of God-given authority to do the following:

- destroy the works of the enemy on earth,
- protect the children of God,
- ensure that righteous verdicts are released upon the earth.

The authority of this Court should be applied in order to establish international businesses and ministries, by obtaining proper mandates, passes for protection, and valid title deeds to procure territory.

This authority should also be exercised in order to assist the Body of Christ in securing all spheres of influence, and to reach the respective summits of each of the mountains or Godly ordained spheres of influence.

Righteous laws, structures, and systems are established through this

Court; while unrighteous governments and rulers are uprooted, according to the will and ways of the Father.

It is also of great importance that international anointing, authorities, and callings are released over the earth, in order to reach those responding to these specific calls of the Lord.

"And Jehoshaphat stood in the congregation of Judah and Jerusalem, in the house of the LORD, before the new court,
And said, O LORD God of our fathers, art not thou God in heaven? and rulest not thou over all the kingdoms of the heathen? and in thine hand is there not power and might, so that none is able to withstand thee?"
2 Chronicles 20:5-7

Fig. 5: The International Court

The Mountains Court

Introduction

"And it shall come to pass in the last days, that the mountain of the LORD'S house shall be established in the top of the mountains, and shall be exalted above the hills; and all nations shall flow unto it.
And many people shall go and say, Come ye, and let us go up to the mountain of the LORD, to the house of the God of Jacob; and he will teach us of his ways, and we will walk in his paths: for out of Zion shall go forth the law, and the word of the LORD from Jerusalem.
And he shall judge among the nations, and shall rebuke many people: and they shall beat their swords into plowshares, and their spears into pruninghooks: nation shall not lift up sword against nation, neither shall they learn war any more."

Isaiah 2:2-4

The book of Isaiah reveals that during the last days, the Body of Christ's jurisdiction of governance will be established in a position of authority within all the various spheres of influence, or mountains.

For the Church to accomplish this, children of God need to mobilise into their respective positions within this Court. The Mountains Court comprises of the following six divisions:

- The Media Mountain Court
- The Arts and Entertainment Mountain Court
- The Governance Mountain Court
- The Economy Mountain Court
- The Education Mountain Court
- The Family Mountain Court

When Christ was crucified for our sins, dominion, rule, and authority were given back to His Church. God is calling His sons and daughters to accept their authorities and positions, and to reclaim their rule on earth.

The aim is most assuredly not to idly wait for the rapture to take place, but to put an asserted effort into taking back what was lost when mankind fell in the Garden of Eden. The ultimate purpose is to reign as the sons and daughters of the most High God on earth.

"Again, the devil taketh him up into an exceeding high mountain, and sheweth him all the kingdoms of the world, and the glory of them; And saith unto him, All these things will I give thee, if thou wilt fall down and worship me."

Matthew 4:8-9

We shall take back sovereign power on earth by taking back rule over the various mountains. Whoever rules these mountains, rules the earth.

Satan is going to fight relentlessly to remain in power. Therefore, God is raising armies across the globe to fight tirelessly in order to conquer in Jesus name and through His power.

We know that God is a God of strategy and to operate within these courts is a crucial part of His strategy. Individual, ministries, businesses, and churches will all work together in the Body of Christ.

If we lose the battle in the spiritual dimension, it will also be lost in the physical dimension. The Spirit of God is therefore revealing strategy to us in these latter days, which was unknown to the Church in the past. God is utilizing the prophetic voice through His prophets on earth to accomplish this.

God's plan and strategies for the various mountains are released through the Mountains Court. The more actively we partake in the court proceedings the more effectively God's will, will be realised. This in turn, will ensure that the standard will be lifted and we will function in much greater success and victory as the Ecclesia on earth.

God implemented the system of the mountains or divisions through which the earth should be governed. Satan did not change this system, nor did he re-invent another, he simply corrupted the system when Adam lost rule over the earth. We deny the enemy dominion by being steadfastly guided in the will and ways of the Father concerning His mountains.

"So shall they fear the name of the LORD from the west, and his glory from the rising of the sun. When the enemy shall come in like a flood, the Spirit of the LORD shall lift up a standard against him."

Isaiah 59:19

Please note that a detailed description of an experience in all the Mountain Courts will be detailed in chapter 4 and will therefore be absent in this section.

Also, all proceedings are conducted within the same building, but different Courtrooms, with the Son of man seated to the right of the Father.

Let us take a brief look at the various Mountains.

The Education Mountain Court

"And the spirit of the Lord shall rest upon him, the spirit of wisdom and understanding, the spirit of counsel and might, the spirit of knowledge and of the fear of the Lord; And shall make him of quick understanding in the fear of the Lord: and he shall not judge after the sight of his eyes, neither reprove after the hearing of his ears:"

Isaiah 11:2-3

In order to understand the Education Mountain Court, it is good to have a basic understanding of the function of the education mountain.

The main objective of this mountain is the following:

- to raise Godly leaders,
- to train and equip His children to successfully take up their positions on each of the mountains,
- to bring wisdom and understanding,
- to reveal Godly instruction,
- to accomplish spiritual maturity, and
- to create Godly educational structures, systems, programmes and material.

General information

- Any person can represent him or herself as well as their families in this Court.
- Any business owner or person in a position of authority to train, equip, and teach within their business can represent that business and everyone that forms part of it.
- Any person standing in a position of authority for the education of a ministry, a country, or nation may intercede in this Court.

An interpretation

The purpose of this mountain is to train and equip people for their God-ordained purposes on whatever mountain they are called to function. Through the education mountain we are to raise a new breed of Godly leaders, as this mountain is polluted by the enemy with false religions as well as false teachings. The mere existence of the Holy Trinity is constantly challenged and questioned.

God wants us to be trained and equipped in Godly wisdom as opposed to the world's attempt to teach people with worldly knowledge. Therefore, God is going to transform this mountain with the Spirit of wisdom and understanding and with the Spirit of knowledge and of the fear of the Lord.

Generations will be taught that the beginning of all wisdom is to fear the Lord. They will have a good understanding to obey God's commandments and will be generations that have learned to worship the King of kings in spirit and in truth.

This will release the movement of God's power on earth.

"The fear of the Lord is the beginning of wisdom: a good understanding have all they that do his commandments: his praise endureth for ever."

Psalm 111:10

God-anointed teachers will influence all spheres of this mountain to instruct in the ways of the Lord. God is using them to break down the deceiving strongholds of the enemy and to restore biblical principles and truth.

The teacher must always abide in the truth, and experience improvement by the Spirit, to be able to bring reformation to the nations.

God is raising His children on this mountain to teach, write, and create new educational material to infiltrate this mountain. This mountain will be occupied by those who stand for the righteous raising and training of Godly leaders. The walls that were erected around this mountain by false teachings and religions will be crushed by His anointed teachers and be replaced by truth and righteousness.

This mountain will be transformed through our successful mediation and intercession within this Court.

The relevance of the Education Mountain Court

- To obtain an impartation of Godly plans and purposes for an individual's, ministry's or nation's calling with regards to this mountain.
- Through the Education Mountain Court, we are also able to obtain passes for protection for ourselves, family members, ministries, and business and to remove barriers pertaining to legal right in educational matters.
- This Court will also need to be frequented to receive educational mandates ordained by God, and to establish the educational mountain in a business, church, community, country or ministry.
- Most importantly, it is through this Court that we ensure that the educational material entering and exiting a specific country or nation is protected.

The Media Mountain Court

"And that they should publish and proclaim in all their cities, and in Jerusalem......"
Nehemiah 8:15

General information

- Any individual can represent him or herself and their families, ministry, business, nation or community according to their jurisdictional right in this court.

An interpretation

This mountain is currently, almost entirely ruled by evil forces, partly because the Church did not recognise the timely importance of the media mountain.

However, God is changing this situation and He wants to use media to be a voice to the world to proclaim His truth, and to bring them timeous warnings. God wants the media to be a voice of virtue, of His kindness, goodness, and to bring hope to nations. The aim is to change the spiritual atmosphere through words of hope and truth that are sowed all over the world by this mountain.

These Holy Spirit-inspired words will be the seed that will be planted in the spirits of God's children who will be planted into nations and will turn the hearts of men and nations back to the Father.

Media is an exceptional tool through which a message may be delivered. Unfortunately, at present, the media is delivering a message of discouragement, hopelessness, and rebellion. This negative message has a direct influence on the morality of a nation.

Through the enduring intercession and mediation of children of God, within this Court, the Kingdom of Light will obtain the right to distribute Kingdom-minded journalists, news reporters, news editors, and evangelists on this mountain by which the Good News can reach all the ends of the earth.

"How beautiful upon the mountains are the feet of him that bringeth good tidings, that publisheth peace; that bringeth good tidings of good, that publisheth salvation; that saith unto Zion, Thy God reigneth!
Thy watchmen shall lift up the voice; with the voice together shall they sing: for they shall see eye to eye, when the Lord shall bring again Zion."

Isaiah 52:7-8

Individuals, organisations, and institutions on the summits of the mountains who are not surrendering to God, will simply be replaced by God. God's will, will be done on earth regardless of human interference.

The relevance

- First and foremost, to receive heavenly authority for this mountain.
- To receive an impartation of the Godly plans and purposes for this mountain according to one's individual, ministry or nations callings.
- To obtain passes for protection for oneself, family members, ministry, or business.
- To remove legal rights from the enemy.
- To receive mandates ordained by God.

- To establish this mountain in a business, church, community, country, or ministry.
- To protect the messages that the media is proclaiming and to release heavenly messages of truth on earth.
- To safeguard media material entering and exiting a specific country or nation.

The Governance Mountain Court

"And I will clothe him with thy robe, and strengthen him with thy girdle, and I will commit thy government into his hand: and he shall be a father to the inhabitants of Jerusalem, and to the house of Judah."

Isaiah 22:21

General information

- The main function of this Court is to serve the other Courts and mountains.
- To ensure that the correct procedures and systems are implemented and followed, and that the verdicts rendered from other courts are implemented.
- This Court stands in a servant position, rather than on a ruling one.
- Any person can represent him or herself and their families, ministry, business, nation or community according to his or her jurisdictional right in this Court.

An interpretation

By having dominion in the governance mountain, the righteous Kingdom of Jesus Christ can be established on earth.

Government in all its forms affect every human activity in many important ways. While Parliaments of the different countries pass laws which affect whole nations, and consequently all the mountains, the enemy is tirelessly working this to his advantage.

The earthly system is governed and ruled from this mountain, however, this is not God's plan. God rules and governs from Mount Zion and the governance mountain is there, only, to assist and serve Mount Zion.

God's governing system will be established on earth when Jesus returns to rule from His throne or seat of governance on Mount Zion, and all governments on earth will submit to His rule.

The governance mountain is a complex and demanding mountain to occupy; and so one should enquire of the Lord, whether one is ordained and called to operate on this mountain. Everyone on this mountain should have gone through a time of preparation in which the Holy Spirit trained and prepared such a person.

Those in the apostolic authority have great influence on this mountain. They are used by the Lord to proclaim righteous statutes in order to transform those governments. God's Kingdom and His government are established on this mountain by engaging in righteous politics and being the authoritative influence of heaven on earth.

God has appointed a multitude of angels, and more specifically, territorial angels working in co-operation with Apostles to achieve what God has called them for, and to prepare the way for the rule of Jesus.

Prophets are raised to bring vision and direction to all mountains. However, the prophetic voice will be so loud in proclaiming to the governmental mountain, it will echo in all dimensions.

The time has come for the eagles to rise on this mountain. The time has also come for God's plans and purposes to be voiced to governments and parliaments. Let the true prophets of the Lord identify and call out to those who stand in the Apostolic anointing, and those who are called and destined to reach the summit of this mountain.

God's intention for a government is for it to be of service to its nation, while being a reflection of God's Kingdom. A government should set an example of Godly principles, by fearing the Lord and by being a blessing to its people.

The biggest obstacle for children of God operating on this mountain is pride, which should be guarded against with vigour. Once you succumb to pride, your DNA is corrupted by the DNA of the enemy; and God Himself, will become your enemy. Therefore, humility will be the greatest method of resistance for God's children, so that they may receive grace to advance to the summit of this mountain.

"But he giveth more grace. Wherefore he saith, God resisteth the proud, but giveth grace unto the humble."

James 4:6

The relevance

- To receive heavenly authority for this mountain.
- To receive an impartation of the Godly plans and purposes for this mountain, according to an individual, ministry, or nations calling.
- To obtain passes for protection for oneself, family members, ministry, or business.
- To remove legal rights from the enemy.
- To receive mandates ordained by God.
- To establish this mountain in a business, church, community, country, or ministry.

- To unlock Godly systems.
- To establish the governance mountain on earth.
- To uproot evil rulers and to establish those ordained and called by God for this mountain, who will serve their nations and its people with a humble and pure heart.
- To establish righteous partnering between governments and to unbind unrighteous partnering.

The Economy Mountain Court

"And be not conformed to this world: but be ye transformed by the renewing of your mind, that ye may prove what is that good, and acceptable, and perfect, will of God. The economy mountain is about prosperity as well as taking and occupying territory for the Kingdom of God."

Romans 12:2

General information

- The other mountains can be empowered through this mountain.
- The main function of this Court is to ensure that wealth or finances are legally released.
- Finances are released to accomplish Kingdom purposes.
- Finances are also released to provide for the Ecclesia.
- There are many treasure chambers within this Court.
- These chambers contain the necessary provision for each family, community, business, nation, or country.
- The keys to the various treasure chambers should be obtained within this court.
- Any individual may represent him or herself and their families, ministry, business, nation or community, according to their jurisdictional right for this Court.

An interpretation

"The LORD shall open unto thee his good treasure, the heaven to give the rain unto thy land in his season, and to bless all the work of thine hand: and thou shalt lend unto many nations, and thou shalt not borrow."

Deuteronomy 28:12

God is opening doors all over the world for Godly ordained businesses. He is also shaking the foundations of this mountain, by restoring His principles for doing business.

Earthly resources, silver and gold (finances), are utilised to strengthen and build His Kingdom. We shall only be successful in conquering this mountain if we are not conformed to this world, but rather, to heaven.

God is raising a new generation of David's, Daniel's and Joseph's to take up their positions as His anointed ones at the summit of this mountain. The Lord is going to use them to do business supernaturally, to the extent, that the supernatural will become natural. Sustained communion in a personal relationship with God is the key to supernatural business.

God is teaching His kings and governors His perspectives on righteousness, integrity, truth, and His heart concerning business and the economy. These are vastly different to the world's perspectives. By doing business supernaturally, common sense will be stupefied and Almighty God will be pleased.

God is using the David's, Joseph's and Daniel's to return the spirit of excellence and integrity to this mountain; which will cause God's children to exceed all others on this mountain.

Once you represent His Kingdom with unshakeable integrity, you will begin to receive authority on this mountain. Excellence provides wealth for the long-term, as excellence is a Kingdom value. This should never be confused with perfectionism, which is a counterfeit, and is inspired by the religious spirit. One of the surest paths to promotion is through being excellent, as Joseph and Daniel were.

"Forasmuch as an excellent spirit, and knowledge, and understanding, interpreting of dreams, and shewing of hard sentences, and dissolving of doubts, were found in the same Daniel, whom the king named Belteshazzar: now let Daniel be called, and he will shew the interpretation."

Daniel 5:12

"And the LORD was with Joseph, and he was a prosperous man; and he was in the house of his master the Egyptian.
And his master saw that the LORD was with him, and that the LORD made all that he did to prosper in his hand."

Genesis 39:2-3

Those in the marketplace who are willing to sacrifice to obtain the rule on this mountain will be met with fierce tests. However, the purpose of these tests, are to qualify them for what is to come.

During what was probably the worst day of his life up to that point, David lost his wife, his children, his possessions, and his troops wanted to stone him. A mere twenty-four later, Saul was dead and David's kingly reign commenced.

God is calling His children not to conform to the worldly system but to trust solely in Him. The economic system of this world, Babylon, will be shaken until it collapses, as God is raising up kings to build a Godly economy in His Kingdom which will function independently from the world.

On this mountain, God's children will be inspired by creative Holy Spirit ideas. This will result in businesses through new inventions of enormous magnitude and influence.

The transfer of wealth from the kingdom of darkness to the Kingdom of Light will be ensured by Godly wisdom, insight, and faith.

The relevance

"The silver is mine, and the gold is mine, saith the LORD of hosts."

Haggai 2:8

- To receive heavenly authority for this mountain.
- To receive impartations of Godly plans and purposes for this mountain according to an individual, ministry or nations calling.
- To obtain passes for protection for oneself, family members, ministry, or business.
- To remove legal rights from the enemy.
- To receive mandates ordained by God to acquire territory.
- To establish this mountain in a business, church, community, country, or ministry.
- To unlock the treasure chambers in heaven.
- To establish the rule of the Kingdom of Light on the economy mountain.
- To expand God's economy on earth.
- To establish righteous partnering between businesses and countries; and to eliminate unrighteous and corrupt partnering.

The Arts and Entertainment Mountain Court

And Miriam the prophetess, the sister of Aaron, took a timbrel in her hand; and all the women went out after her with timbrels and with dances."

Exodus 15:20

General information

- This Court resembles an image of heavenly culture.
- Any individual may represent him or herself and their families, ministry, business, nation or community, according to their jurisdictional right for this Court.

An interpretation

Following Israel's crossing of the Red Sea, the Israelites celebrated their newfound freedom from slavery in joyful dance and prayer, led by Miriam. Dancing, music and feasts were the order of the day in biblical times, having been ordained by God. We are to glorify God through arts and entertainment and thereby strengthen communion and unity among the brethren.

"These are the feasts of the LORD, even holy convocations, which ye shall proclaim in their seasons."

Leviticus 23:4

The first mention of art in the Bible is in the book of Exodus chapter thirty-one. Moses was instructed to build a tabernacle in which to house the Ark of the Covenant. This tabernacle was beautified by God-appointed and anointed artisans with inspired artistic skills.

"... and in the hearts of all that are wise hearted I have put wisdom, that they may make all that I have commanded thee;"

Exodus 31:6b

Art originated from God as it is He who blesses and anoints us with artistic skills.

"But thou art holy, O thou that inhabitest the praises of Israel."

Psalm 22:3

Our praise and worship is a powerful weapon of advancement in which God delights. King David understood the power in praise and worship as he always sent out the worshipers ahead of the armies before commencing battle.

"And when he had consulted with the people, he appointed singers unto the LORD, and that should praise the beauty of holiness, as they went out before the army, and to say, Praise the LORD; for his mercy endureth for ever.
And when they began to sing and to praise, the LORD set ambushments against the children of Ammon, Moab, and mount Seir, which were come against Judah; and they were smitten."

2 Chronicles 20:21-22

Holy Spirit-inspired arts and entertainment in all its various forms, is a prophetic voice released over the earth.
God uses this voice to bring messages to His Church. We should be attentive to these in order for us to get an understanding of the movements of God on earth. Godly-inspired arts and entertainment releases a heavenly culture on earth.

The relevance

- To receive heavenly authority for this mountain.
- To receive an impartation of the Godly plans and purposes for this mountain according to one's calling.
- To obtain passes for protection for oneself, family members, ministry, and business.
- To remove legal rights from the enemy.
- To receive mandates ordained by God for Holy Spirit-inspired creativity and skill.
- To establish this mountain in a business, church, community, country, or ministry.
- To release a prophetic voice in order to establish a heavenly culture on earth.

The Family Mountain Court

"Then one said unto him, Behold, thy mother and thy brethren stand without, desiring to speak with thee.
But he answered and said unto him that told him, Who is my mother? and who are my brethren?
And he stretched forth his hand toward his disciples, and said, Behold my mother and my brethren!
For whosoever shall do the will of my Father which is in heaven, the same is my brother, and sister, and mother."

Matthew 12:47-50

General information

- The main function of this Court is to keep the Body of Christ together as one unified family.
- In this Court families and tribes are represented.
- Each family bears a specific anointing and authority.

An interpretation

"One of his disciples, Andrew, Simon Peter's brother, saith unto him,
There is a lad here, which hath five barley loaves, and two small fishes: but what are they among so many?
And Jesus said, Make the men sit down. Now there was much grass in the place. So the men sat down, in number about five thousand.
And Jesus took the loaves; and when he had given thanks, he distributed to the disciples, and the disciples to them that were set down; and likewise of the fishes as much as they would."

John 6:8-11

The focus of this mountain is to nurture, care for and to sustain individuals and their families. This mountain is mainly divided into two different sections namely: Household and Welfare.

In the Household section the following are focus points:

- social and pastoral services through pastoral care,
- marriage counselling and courses,
- ministry to children and teenagers,
- spiritual and pastoral counselling to all ages,
- ministry to the sick and bereaved and,
- nurturing new believers.

The Welfare section focuses on:

- food schemes for local and foreign communities,
- community outreach projects to support the sick, elderly, widows, orphans, prisoners, the homeless and broken persons,
- to assist and support communities in times of crises, caused by natural disasters, for example.

It is important to reiterate that this mountain renders a service to both the local community and the broader public. Therefore, the focus is on offering a service and to supply the needs of the local and the broader community.

It is imperative for businesses to understand the importance of the welfare of their families, and to love and care for them. Business owners often overlook this importance on purpose, as it is viewed as an unaffordable expense that causes unprofitability.

God expects His anointed rulers and leaders to rule over their respective communities with undeniable compassion and endearment.

The relevance

"And if it seem evil unto you to serve the LORD, choose you this day whom ye will serve; whether the gods which your fathers served that were on the other side of the flood, or the gods of the Amorites, in whose land ye dwell: but as for me and my house, we will serve the LORD."

Joshua 24:15

- To obtain heavenly mandates for specific families, tribes, and communities.
- The protection of families, tribes, and communities.
- Provision for families, tribes, and communities.

The Supreme Court

"After this I looked, and, behold, a door was opened in heaven: and the first voice which I heard was as it were of a trumpet talking with me; which said, Come up hither, and I will shew thee things which must be hereafter.
And immediately I was in the spirit: and, behold, a throne was set in heaven, and one sat on the throne.
And he that sat was to look upon like a jasper and a sardine stone: and there was a rainbow round about the throne, in sight like unto an emerald.
And round about the throne were four and twenty seats: and upon the seats I saw four and twenty elders sitting, clothed in white raiment; and they had on their heads crowns of gold.
And out of the throne proceeded lightnings and thunderings and voices: and there were seven lamps of fire burning before the throne, which are the seven Spirits of God.
And before the throne there was a sea of glass like unto crystal: and in the midst of the throne, and round about the throne, were four beasts full of eyes before and behind."

Revelation 4:1-6

General information

- This is the Court with the highest authority.
- This Court is not housed in a building, but is situated in the indescribable landscape of eternal space.
- Mount Zion is the place of governmental rule over all the earth.
- The kingdom of darkness may not be represented in this Court, as they have no right to influence any decisions made in this Court.
- You have to stand in an intimate relationship with the Father in order to reach the summit of this Mountain.
- It is possible for all God's children to reach the summit through Christ Jesus.

- Of all His council, the Elders around God's throne have the highest authority.
- The Day of Judgement, referred to in Revelation chapter 20, shall take place from this Court.
- This is a place of rule, judgement, and worship.
- There are a multitude of angels and people in this Court, more than in any of the other Courts.
- Jesus is seated on a throne to the right of God.
- In this Court He is God, the Alpha and the Omega, the King of kings and the Lord of lords.

"Saying, I am Alpha and Omega, the first and the last: and, What thou seest, write in a book, and send it unto the seven churches which are in Asia; unto Ephesus, and unto Smyrna, and unto Pergamos, and unto Thyatira, and unto Sardis, and unto Philadelphia, and unto Laodicea.
And I turned to see the voice that spake with me. And being turned, I saw seven golden candlesticks;
And in the midst of the seven candlesticks one like unto the Son of man, clothed with a garment down to the foot, and girt about the paps with a golden girdle.
His head and his hairs were white like wool, as white as snow; and his eyes were as a flame of fire;
And his feet like unto fine brass, as if they burned in a furnace; and his voice as the sound of many waters.
And he had in his right hand seven stars: and out of his mouth went a sharp twoedged sword: and his countenance was as the sun shineth in his strength.
And when I saw him, I fell at his feet as dead. And he laid his right hand upon me, saying unto me, Fear not; I am the first and the last:
I am he that liveth, and was dead; and, behold, I am alive for evermore, Amen; and have the keys of hell and of death."

Revelation 1:11-18

An experience

"After completing the "The Code of Law of our Kingdom" found in Chapter 2, we received the instruction from the Holy Spirit to access this Court in order to bind and approve this Code within the highest authority.

This is strategic, as any verdict delivered from this Court will naturally carry a higher authority than any of the other Courts. It means that it has the power to overrule any law given by any government on earth as it is there to protect the kingdoms on earth from the works of the anti-Christ spirit.

"And every spirit that confesseth not that Jesus Christ is come in the flesh is not of God: and this is that spirit of antichrist, whereof ye have heard that it should come; and even now already is it in the world."

1 John 4:3

As we entered into this Court, my physical body felt like it was about to explode. It felt like all the blood was rushing to my head, and I could barely keep upright. The atmosphere and the presence of God was extremely overwhelming.

Although, I saw the Throne of God, I could not see God Himself as a thick cloud surrounded Him. Jesus Christ was seated on the right, next to God the Father, and was dressed and crowned as the King of all kings and the Lord of all lords.

I had an overwhelming desire to move closer to Him, especially as I sensed the vast spaces present. The magnitude of this reality, almost made God feel somewhat distant to my fallible nature.

I then started to become more aware of our surroundings. It felt and looked like, we were standing in the farthest reaches of outer space, somewhere in the middle of the universe, with a bottomless floor extending into the depths of eternity.

I also became aware of mountains surrounding us with a horizon reflecting the colours of the setting sun, despite there being no sun present. I knew the time was 18:00 and this was of particular significance as the Lord had recently revealed to me in a dream that we were soon going to have to move into a new season.

I saw an angel holding the four corners of the wind, and became aware of other natural elements such as infinite streams of water, lightning, snow, and hail. The best way to describe this, is that it appeared as if God was collecting all the lighting, snow, and hail.

I also saw twenty-four smaller thrones, surrounding God's throne, and on these the Elders were seated, representing God's Supreme Council.

We were accompanied by David, Ezekiel, Esther, and Paul. David, Ezekiel and Esther were there as witnesses for us, whilst Paul was there to witness the fruit of his work on earth. Roughly 40% of all the scripture we used in The Code of Law, was written by Paul and we were aware that he wanted to witness the manifestation of the sons of God. I was humbly amused by Paul's inquisitive nature.

It is noteworthy to add that there were copious amounts of joy, peace, and righteousness among all those before us, without any trace whatsoever of tension, fear, or impatience.

I was astounded to learn that God consulted with His Supreme Council; which serves to emphasize the gravity of His righteousness. In spite of being the all-powerful Creator of the universe, He does not reign independently from the Body of Christ.

Although I could not see them, I was aware of thousands of angels surrounding us, and continually singing God's praises. I also saw a multitude of angels delivering new praises every time they circled God's throne.

My attention was then drawn to a particular person within the Supreme Council. He was intensely engaged in a conversation with God, but I did not know what he was saying or who he was at that point in time. I enquired of the Holy Spirit regarding this person, and the Holy Spirit revealed to me that every Elder specialised in something specific during their time on earth. This Elder was a specialist on legislation, and through another experience the following day, the Lord revealed to me, that this Elder had indeed been Moses.

We were then asked of the Lord what the motives of our hearts were. I knew the Lord was already familiar with our true motives and that the right answer would be to remain truthful and sincere. The true test was to reveal an honest heart.

An angel presented The Code of Law in the form of a written scroll, and Jesus sealed it with His ring, and proclaimed His will to bring His Kingdom to earth. Instinctively, I replied with the words: *"Our Father which art in heaven, hallowed be thy name. Thy Kingdom come. Thy will be done in earth, as it is in heaven."*

Our experience was sealed with the assuring words of the Lord that many will be able to build on the foundations that were laid this day.

"Great is the Lord, and greatly to be praised in the city of our God, in the mountain of his holiness.
Beautiful for situation, the joy of the whole earth, is mount Zion, on the sides of the north, the city of the great King."

Psalm 48:1-2

An interpretation

"But ye are come unto mount Sion, and unto the city of the living God, the heavenly Jerusalem, and to an innumerable company of angels,"

Hebrews 12:22

King David ruled his kingdom from Jerusalem with the highest hill being Mount Zion. He built the Temple and placed the Ark of the Covenant on Mount Zion, where God dwelt in the midst of His people. This was also a place of worship and judgement (See *Exodus 25:22 and 1 Chronicles 16:4-27).*

Mount Zion was very significant due to both the throne of the king and the Ark of the Covenant being there. The throne was the seat of authority, rule, and judgement; while the Ark was a place of worship and the presence of God's glory.

Scriptures emphasises and reveals the great importance of the throne and the Ark in Zion.

Those who come to the spiritual Mount Zion will know God and will not be a people who have merely familiarised themselves regarding Him. As the Psalmist emphasises:

"In Judah God is known, His name is great in Israel. In Salem also is His tabernacle, and His dwelling place in Zion."

Psalm 76:2

King David foretold that the Messiah would reign from Zion. Just as King David ruled over his great empire from Zion; even so the Lord Jesus, the Son of David, will rule from Zion. Every year, the nations of the earth will send their delegations to Jerusalem to worship the King of kings and the Lord of lords.

"And it shall come to pass, that every one that is left of all the nations which came against Jerusalem shall even go up from year to year to worship the King, the LORD of hosts, and to keep the feast of tabernacles.

And it shall be, that whoso will not come up of all the families of the earth unto Jerusalem to worship the King, the LORD of hosts, even upon them shall be no rain."

Zechariah 14:16-17

Once again, the earthly Mount Zion is a reflection of the heavenly Mount Zion, which is the centre of the throne of God.

Regardless of which Courtroom you are interceding and mediating in, you will always be looking to the same throne. This is the Court closest to God's throne, and therefore the highest in authority. The closer you move to God, the higher the level of authority you will be entrusted with.

"The LORD hath prepared his throne in the heavens; and his kingdom ruleth over all."

Psalm 103:19

Each of the assemblies of Mount Zion, comprising every Church that is enduring in holiness and faithful in their higher callings, will be covered with His glory *(Isaiah 4:3-6)*. The Lord will exalt His Church to great authority and glory, to help prepare the way for the Second Coming of Christ.

The relevance

To declare that we do not even remotely begin to comprehend the significance and importance of this Court is an understatement, as infinite wisdom in this regard is yet to be obtained. Nevertheless, the following can and should be noted:

- It is most important for every child of God to reach the summit of Mount Zion through their personal relationship with the Father.
- Any law implemented on earth, regardless of its nature, should be established in the spiritual realm through this Court.
- Unrighteous laws and governments should be uprooted and destroyed from any position of authority in this Court.
- The Ecclesia should govern the earth, with Christ in the ruling position.
- The Ecclesia should enthusiastically partake in the proceedings and councils within this Court.
- Verdicts and judgements released from this Court will have an influence on the other Court proceedings; and will fortify those cases presented in righteousness according to the sovereign will

of God.

- Heavenly mandates should be released through the Ecclesia from this Court.
- According to the guidance of the Holy Spirit, authorities that influence the world can be obtained through this Court.

Fig. 6: The Supreme Court

Fig. 7: Diagram of the Seven Heavenly Courts from Above

4

THE DAY OF ABUNDANCE

The following is an account of an experience we had while establishing a new business, and how we were guided by the Holy Spirit to navigate through all the Courts in a single session:

"(A Psalm of praise.) Make a joyful noise unto the LORD, all ye lands.
Serve the LORD with gladness: come before his presence with singing.
Know ye that the LORD he is God: it is he that hath made us, and not we ourselves; we are his people, and the sheep of his pasture.
Enter into his gates with thanksgiving, and into his courts with praise: be thankful unto him, and bless his name.
For the LORD is good; his mercy is everlasting; and his truth endureth to all generations."

Psalm 100

As the Psalmist emphasized, we started with praise and worship in order to get into the Father's presence.

The first Court we entered into was the Court of Mercy and Grace. This is usually the Court you will commence with, as this is the Court supplying the grace one needs, to enter into the other Courts.

Standing in front of the Throne of Mercy and Grace, we asked God to reveal any legitimate right the enemy possessed against this business.

The Lord emphasised the curses and rituals that were performed by occult groups in the beginning of this decade. We were then led by the Holy Spirit to break their powers through prayer.

Besides this, the blessings and prayers of the Saints testified as defence, as these were spoken on behalf of the ministries and Godly businesses that were ordained to be birthed during this same decade.

After this, we were prompted by the Holy Spirit to enter into the Supreme Court, and in obedience we asked the following of the Lord, within this Court:

- that the power of our written Code of Law for our kingdom, would manifest,
- that the barriers of defence created by the Code of Law would apply to this business,
- that the Lord's personal declaration pertaining to this business be imparted to our spirits,
- that the mandates for every mountain be released over us, according to the will and purposes of the Lord.

One of the Elders from the Supreme Council, Daniel, then signed all the relevant mandates, by which permission was granted for these to be released.

I stood in absolute awe at Daniel's kind-heartedness, amazed at how I was able to discern his spirit. This was made possible through the gift of discernment by the Holy Spirit, which is discussed in the book of *1 Corinthians* in chapter 12.

From Mount Zion, we went into the Economy Mountain Court.

This Court displays wealth and royalty as all the people present, wore royal garments, and it was evident that all the silver and gold belonged to God and have been created by Him to achieve His purposes.

It was brought to our attention that it is not the silver and gold (money) which is corrupt, but rather the love of it. All the focus was on Jesus Christ, as His Glory overshadowed all the riches and wealth surrounding us. We understood that the moment you remove your focus from Christ and focus on earthly riches, you will be consumed by it.

I became aware of an innumerable amount of treasure chambers allocated to specific individuals, families, businesses, countries, ministries, and churches. This was God's provision for His people. He is the good Father Who has already made provision for His children even before they were created.

Under the guidance of the Spirit of God, I intuitively knew that we were supposed to obtain the keys for these treasure chambers in order to unlock God's provisions.

Copies of the keys were handed to ourselves as well as other designated people. This was done to distribute the risk, as well as to keep the Body of Christ dependant. Entrusting only one person with such an important key would have made it far too easy for the enemy to attempt to steal the provision. Therefore, the burden is distributed, making it lighter.

Suddenly, Abraham, appeared, politely requesting permission to address God and the Court. In humility, he continued to request the Lord that the same blessing of provision that was bestowed upon him, be released over us. We were moved by his generous and genuine gesture, to advance the Kingdom of God on earth.

From the Economy Mountain Court, we proceeded into the Family Mountain Court. The people present were grouped in families or clans. And judging by the way they were dressed it was clear that each family possessed a certain authority and anointing.

The laughter of children echoed throughout this Courtroom. Together with all the happiness and joy present, it was overwhelming. There are no orphans in heaven, and even if a child on earth dies without any family, that child is welcomed into his or her heavenly family clan. To be loved and nurtured by this family, the way God intended.

We requested the Lord for the gates to be opened, for the God-ordained families to move into this business. We also interceded on behalf of the families, for their protection and prayed that the ordained families be bound together by love.

An elder or father, representing each family in the spiritual realm, stood up, and blessed the families in this business, with their respective authorities and anointing. It was an extraordinary gesture of love, reflecting the Father's heart.

From here, we continued on to the Governance Court. This Court can only be described as a room with incomprehensible depth.
The people inside this Court all wore very humble garments, and it struck us how far removed these servants were from the earthly glamour of politics.

One of the seven Spirits of God, the Spirit of Counsel, was released over this business though the Governance Court, and we asked the Lord for His perfect governance to be released over this business. In addition, heavenly strategy and procedure were also imparted to us, by the Lord.

From being actively present in this Court, we knew that its core function was to serve the other Courts and to ensure that systems and procedures were implemented and maintained to keep everything well-governed.

The Education Court followed, and upon entering, I was awestruck. I saw an infinite amount of words filling the entire space, formulating sentences, telling a specific story. The Holy Spirit revealed that this is revelation knowledge being revealed to God's children, and that all revelation knowledge put together, tells a story. Whenever you receive revelation knowledge from the Lord, only a word or a sentence of the entire story as a whole, is revealed to you.

Again, this proves the importance of the Body of Christ working together and that we cannot function independently. In order to be able to comprehend the bigger picture, it is important that we integrate everything we receive from the Lord.

We requested that the scroll of this business be imparted to the spirits of the people ordained by God, to occupy the Education Mountain for this business. This greatly assists in the complete plan of God to be written on their hearts.

Angels were standing by, with bags filled with seed which they hurried to plant, being seeds of wisdom, understanding and of knowledge into the spirits of those who are called for the Education Mountain of this business. This assists in preparing those to come.

The blue print on how education should function within this business was released to us, and this will assist in edifying the four walls of the business (family, clients, territory and employees). This in turn, guarantees sustainable growth.

After this, we entered the Arts and Entertainment Court. It took me a few moments to take in everything I saw. There were all sorts of art and entertainment taking place simultaneously, all in perfect harmony.

This Court carries a manifestation of heavenly culture, with the culture on earth being released through this Court.

We were guided by the Holy Spirit to request that the Spirit and voice of prophecy be released through this Court over this business. This was done in order for the prophetic voice to create a culture of strength and power in this business.

From there we visited the Media Mountain Court. Since Media is a voice, proclaiming a message, it is echoed in the spiritual realm. This Court is an aggregation of voices, whose main objective it is to ensure that a wholesome image of God, reflecting hope and truth, is displayed.

Led by the Holy Spirit, we requested the Lord for favour in the world of business, and to reveal to us Godly strategy regarding the marketing of this company.

An angel of the Lord then erected a huge notice in space, visible to all, declaring that this business was birthed from the Kingdom of God.

This was certainly an extraordinary way for the Lord to reveal a specific message to the known world, and we were grateful to have been a part of it.

As we concluded with the Mountains Court we were approaching a state of exhaustion, as our physical bodies felt the strain, from everything our spirits had endured due to this experience.

In spite of this fatigue, we eagerly entered the International Court. We requested from the Lord to release the international mandates, the correct passes for protection and the valid title deeds to obtain territory.

A person representing the kingdom of darkness objected to our request, but was immediately overruled by God. This was made possible, since we had already obtained the right to present these requests in the Supreme Court.

The representative of the kingdom of darkness was obviously not aware of what had transpired in the other Courts, and this was also to our advantage.

Much to our delight, the relevant mandates, title deeds, and passes were granted, and handed over to us.

From the International Court we appeared in the Court of Times and Seasons.

In this Court we pleaded for God to straighten the path of this business. We supplicated for the Lord to be in possession of every time-gate, and also for this business to progress within the

God-ordained times and seasons, and to be blessed with the DNA of Christ Jesus.

Keys, controlling the time-gates, were handed to us, and angels were appointed to assist with guarding these gates.

Following our appearance in the Court of Times and Seasons we progressed to the Parliamentary Court.

In this Court we requested the Lord to obtain passes, which would allow this business to move across borders.

I could see various flags being held by people representing their respective countries. I knew the possibility existed that these flags would not necessarily look exactly like the actual ones on earth, due to the unrighteous symbols on some of them. Like everything else on earth, the design of a flag is either inspired by the Holy Spirit, the enemy, or the human spirit.

Some of those representing the Kingdom of God came forward and planted their flags in the ground. I realised that this gesture meant that as ambassadors of their countries, they granted us permission to obtain territory in their respective countries, permitting us to expand across their borders.

These ambassadors are driven by their passion for God and for His Kingdom to be established on earth. Their perfect love did not seek to advance their own agenda, but rather, the agenda of the One whom they love.

The last Court we entered into, was the Court of the Council of Judges.

Once inside, God granted the opportunity for a judgement to be released over this business. Judgements are positive for those who walk righteously and upright before the face of God.

In full view of the entire congregation surrounding us, a judgement was delivered that this business will honour God, and will build the Kingdom of God.

It is an indescribable honour and blessing to serve the Creator of the Universe through Whose Spirit we received this concession to be part of such a marvellous experience. To have been privileged to visit all the Heavenly Courts in one day, was truly an act of abundance that we sincerely appreciated.

It is our hope and prayer that more children of God will make use of this awesome gift and experience the liberation available through the Heavenly Courts.

All the praise be unto the Holy Trinity!

"Praise ye the Lord. Praise God in his sanctuary: praise him in the firmament of his power.
Praise him for his mighty acts: praise him according to his excellent greatness."

Psalm 150:1-2

EPILOGUE

In the parable of The Sower in Matthew chapter thirteen, you are confronted with what type of seed you represent.

Are you the seed that falls on the footpath and are pecked by the birds? In other words, are you the one hearing God's Divine Message of His Kingly reign, but not understanding it?

Could you be the seed that falls on stony places with no depth, that take root easily due to the shallowness of the soil, but are scorched by the sun? Meaning, could you be the ones who receive the Message with gladness, but only remain standing for a while, and as soon as your faith is tested through tribulation and persecution you continue in your comfortable and familiar earthly ways?

Are you possibly the seed that falls among the thorns, and so when the thorns spring up, the corn is choked? Meaning are you possibly the ones who heard and understood the Message, but remain fruitless due to the multiple worries you succumb to in your lives, and the temptations brought about by your feverish searches for earthly riches?

Or indeed, are you the seed that fell on the good soil, and bear multiple harvests? They are the ones who heard and understood the Message and are persevering through utter obedience and love for the Father. These are the ones who will reap the rewards for what they have sowed.

Those of you who belong to this last category, will achieve great victory, as it is intended by the Lord, that His Heavenly Courts, be navigated by

His true and faithful warriors in Christ.

"And then shall many be offended, and shall betray one another, and shall hate one another. And many false prophets shall rise, and shall deceive many.
And because iniquity shall abound, the love of many shall wax cold.
But he that shall endure unto the end, the same shall be saved."

Matthew 24:10-13

The measure we apply, whether spiritual knowledge and insight through teachings and writings are truly inspired, will always be the Word of God. The wonderfully revealing Word of God should always be the only standard by which we justify any revelation knowledge, and we are to be vigilant and watchful with our adversary being cunning beyond human understanding.

"And they that be wise shall shine as the brightness of the firmament; and they that turn many to righteousness as the stars for ever and ever.
But thou, Daniel, shut up the words, and seal the book, even to the time of the end: many shall run to and fro, and knowledge shall be increased."

Daniel 12:3-4

The enemy is resisting a breakthrough in the multiplication of spiritual knowledge by sowing complacency. People are satisfied with their spiritual lives and are resisting urges to grow any further. In part, this is caused, by their lack of spiritual knowledge, besides their fear to engage the unknown.

"Behold, I stand at the door, and knock: if any man hear my voice, and open the door, I will come in to him, and will sup with him, and he with me."

Revelation 3:20

Although many spiritual leaders may be to blame for the spiritual shortcomings in the children of God, ultimately, the child of God will be held responsible due to his or her own complacent relationship with the Father. Your relationship, remains your responsibility. Thankfully, through the guidance of the Holy Spirit, this is a joyous journey of personal and divine discovery.

"But without faith it is impossible to please him: for he that cometh to God must believe that he is, and that he is a rewarder of them that diligently seek him."

Hebrews 11:6

Mankind's purpose in life, is to glorify God in everything we do, from what we consider to be mundane, to the most important. The latter includes:

- To praise and worship Almighty God as the only living and ever-faithful God.
- Receiving eternal salvation through His only begotten Son, Jesus Christ, Who suffered unbearably on the Cross, so that we may be able to receive redemption for our sins.
- To be eagerly willing to completely surrender to the Creator, so that His omnipotence can be revealed through our unfailing trust in Him.

"For this cause we also, since the day we heard it, do not cease to pray for you, and to desire that ye might be filled with the knowledge of his will in all wisdom and spiritual understanding;
That ye might walk worthy of the Lord unto all pleasing, being fruitful in every good work, and increasing in the knowledge of God;
Strengthened with all might, according to his glorious power, unto all patience and

longsuffering with joyfulness;"

Colossians 1:9-11

God's Kingdom is essentially built and established through each and every single soul obediently following His plan and purposes for each one. These plans and purposes are divinely crafted so that we, as a chosen people, may attain the ultimate glorification in the Holy Trinity.

May the mighty children of the Light, be led by the Holy Spirit, to obediently and patiently wait in the safety and comfort of the eternal Light of His presence.

As the crown of His creation, we should therefore bear our daily cross with boldness.

"Grace and peace be multiplied unto you through the knowledge of God, and of Jesus our Lord."

2 Peter 1:2

REFERENCES

- *Dake's Annotated Reference Bible* by Finis Jennings Dake. Forty-four Printing – May 2013

- *Kingdom Watcher* email article by on www.kingwatch.co.nz – August 2016

- *Times and Seasons* - blog article by Jennifer LeClaire in Charisma Magazine – August 2016

- *Time of your life* - You tube teaching by Andy Stanley – August 2016

APPRECIATION

We recognize Robert Henderson for the work he has done pertaining to the Heavenly Courts, as this proved to be most helpful during our experiences within the Heavenly Courts. Especially concerning some of the interpretations.

We also acknowledge Johnny Enlow for the book he wrote: *The Seven Mountain Prophecy: Unveiling the Coming Elijah Revolution.*

In addition, we recognize Martin van der Merwe and the prophetic books he wrote, which were particularly helpful in gaining prophetic insight into some of the revelations imparted by the Holy Spirit.

We sincerely thank the team from Haima Christou Ministries for their enduring support and assistance. We also acknowledge the following books written and distributed by them: *International Guarding and Operations and Training: A Prayer Strategy*, as well as *Introduction to Spiritual Counselling.*

We acknowledge the official online website of the Kings James Bible for the 1611 Authorised Version of the Holy Scripture for text extracts quoted throughout this publication.

To the best of our ability we've tried to recognise all the sources we consulted and used. However, if we have recorded any information without giving the proper recognition, kindly draw this to our attention and we will seek to correct this in future issues, as it is not our intention to fail to pay recognition, where such recognition is due.

Made in the USA
Monee, IL
11 December 2019

18418231R00157